Where is God?

Auschwitz-Birkenau to Dachau

1942 to 1945

Samuel Althaus

All Rights Reserved. Copyright © 2000 Samuel Althaus

No part of this book may be reproduced or transmitted in any form or by any means, graphic, electronic, or mechanical, including photocopying, recording, taping or by any information storage or retrieval system, without the permission in writing from the author.

Cover illustration © 2000 B. Basnight

ISBN: 0-9712172-0-3

Contents

Dedication	4
Acknowledgement	5
Foreword	6
Part One: BEFORE THE WAR	7
Part Two: THE INVASION	37
Part Three: AUSCHWITZ-BIRKENAU	57
Part Four: DACHAU	122
Part Five: LIBERATION	136
Part Six: EPILOGUE	156

Dedication

This book is dedicated to the memory of my parents, Herschel and Ita Altus, my brothers, Yussel, Srulek and Leibel, my sisters, Chaia and Feigel, my uncle, Leibel Altus, my other relatives and friends from Ciechanow, Poland, and the millions of other innocent victims who were murdered in cold blood in Nazi concentration camps during World War II.

I am also dedicating this book to my brother Simon, cousin Irving, and the other prisoners who managed, by a combination of luck and cleverness, to survive those terrible years during which monstrous evil reigned supreme throughout much of Europe.

I offer my everlasting gratitude to the brave American soldiers who defeated Hitler and liberated from the camps those of us who survived the horrors of the Holocaust.

Acknowledgements

Since my liberation from Dachau in 1945, I intended to write of my experiences during the Holocaust but always found reasons not to do it. Perhaps, deep in my soul, I did not want to confront the demons of Auschwitz/Birkenau and Dachau. It wasn't until late in 1997 that a good friend, who had made several previous offers to help with the book, finally said, "Sam, if you're really serious about writing your book, it's time to get going. I will set aside a couple of mornings each week to interview you on tape and then transcribe the tapes on my computer. We'll start on it tomorrow morning." I knew that he probably would not offer again, so the next morning I showed up at his office and started talking. This book is the result of those lengthy and sometimes very painful talks.

To my good friend, Andrew M. Casey, I say "thank you" for your patience, understanding and wholehearted support during this very emotional project.

I also express deep appreciation to my dear friend, Kathleen Anderson, for her excellent suggestions.

You have made this book a reality, and I thank you from the bottom of my heart.

"HOLOCAUST"

The word invokes nightmares of physical and psychological terror, absolute despair, contemptible indignities, unimaginable atrocities, total degradation, innumerable physical beatings and cold-blooded murders committed against Jews and other peoples for no reason other than their birth or their beliefs.

As a survivor of the Nazi death camps at Auschwitz/Birkenau and Dachau, I need to share my memories and nightmares of those years with future generations.

It is my hope that our civilization will never forget how a diabolical plot to eliminate Jews from the face of the earth, the so-called "Final Solution," almost succeeded.

This book is not intended to be a definitive study of the Holocaust. Rather, it is simply a narrative of my personal experiences and recollections before, during and after one of the most tragic periods in the history of the world and serves as a reminder to future generations that absolute evil, if unchecked, can rise again.

PART ONE

BEFORE THE WAR

The Altus Family

For more than two hundred years before my birth, the Altus family lived and prospered in Ciechanow, a city about fifty kilometers north of Warsaw, Poland, not far from the East Prussian border.

I, Samuel Altus, was born into that family on Friday, October 26, 1924, the fifth son of Herschel and Ita Altus. I was among the Altus family's third-generation to happily live in Ciechanow.

My father, Hershel, was a devoted husband and father who worked long hours at his business to provide the necessities of life for our family. An average-size man, about 5-foot-6-inches tall, he had light brown hair and blue eyes like the sea.

He was a modern man who took a keen interest in what was happening in the world, but his life and ours were deeply rooted in the ancient rituals and beliefs inherent in the Jewish faith.

Our religion prescribed the activities of our daily lives. Early each morning, before going to work at the family poultry business, my father placed his prayer shawl over his shoulders and retreated to a corner of the room for daily prayers. He believed deeply in his religion and always tried to comply with the strict tenets of his faith.

He and my mother kept a kosher home, and our meals were always prepared according to the rules of kosher.

My mother, Ita, whose maiden name was also Altus, supported him in everything. A slender, pretty woman, she had pale blue eyes and straight blond hair that she wore up in back. She was dedicated to raising her children with high morals and a positive outlook on life, and while she could neither read nor write, she insisted that all her children learn how.

Her illiteracy did not mean she was stupid. She was one of the smartest people in my life. She spoke three languages, as did everyone else in the family: Yiddish, for talking with family and friends; Polish, the language used in public school and with Polish friends and businessmen; and Hebrew, used during religious services and in Hebrew school. Later I became fluent in German, Russian, and of course, English, after coming to America.

My mother also knew all the classical music. She listened to symphonies whenever she could ... and operas. She had a lovely, lilting voice, and we often would stop to listen to her sing her favorite pieces, the soft, sweet notes drifting through the open window to the garden outside where we played.

All my brothers and I had light brown hair and blue eyes like my father.

My oldest brother, Yussell, at about 5-feet, 11-inches, was much taller than father, though. He was nine years older than I was, so by the time I started school, he had finished his studies and was working with my father in the poultry business.

Likewise, Srulek, who was seven years older, was considered grown and had begun working with father by the time I started school. He also was tall, at 5-feet, 10-inches, and had the Altus hair and eyes.

Simon, who was five years older, and Leibel, just two years older, were in school when I started. Of course, Simon finished long before Leibel and I, leaving all the household chores to us while he and my brothers worked with father outside the home.

My sister, Chaia was born four years after me, and being the only daughter — for a few years at least — quickly became the darling of the family. Chaia was the most beautiful child I had ever seen. Her soft golden hair shone and her eyes, pale blue like our mother's, sparkled when she smiled. Petite and pretty, she was fastidious about her appearance almost from the day she was born. She hated to get dirty and played in such a way that she never would have to.

My baby sister, Feigel, was just the opposite. Chaia was three when Feigel was born, all dark hair and eyes and an energy that could not be contained. She was a very lively addition to our family and kept us busy trying to keep up with her. She was somewhat of a tomboy who, unlike Chaia, didn't mind getting dirty at all.

Hundreds of people made up our extended family — aunts, uncles, cousins and grandparents on both my father's and mother's side — all of whom lived nearby and interacted with us daily. I'm not sure of the exact figure, but I believe that nearly 10,000 Jews lived in Ciechanow prior to the Nazi occupation.

Many of them were family.

I remember well my maternal grandmother, who had a small baking oven in her home that she used to make matzos for Passover. She never used that particular oven for other types of baking. In preparation for the Passover holidays, she hired a few people to help her roll the dough and bake it, insisting that the religious rituals be strictly followed throughout the matzo baking process.

My paternal grandmother, actually my father's stepmother, was well known throughout our community because she had made several trips throughout Western Europe. For us Jews it was considered something special if you were able to travel to Warsaw, never mind to some other country.

She and my other grandparents died of natural causes before the Holocaust and were buried in the Jewish cemetery in Ciechanow. I have not been back to Poland since the war, but I have learned that the cemetery still exists in a wooded area outside of the town. There is nothing to mark the cemetery and no gravestones remain, but there are people in the village who remember it and have documented its existence.

My two oldest brothers, who worked with my father, sometimes joined him for morning prayers. We were observant but not fanatical, and sometimes, as kids do, we tested the religious rules just for the fun of it.

The most mischievous thing I remember any of us ever doing was the day Leibel and one of his friends saw the shoemaker's wife place a cooked goose in a pan on her windowsill to cool. They crept outside her window and stole the goose. It wasn't that they were hungry or mean, they did it just to have some fun. I don't know if the shoemaker's wife ever figured out what happened to her goose that day.

Another neighbor had goats in her yard. Occasionally, my friends and I sneaked into her yard and milked them. Then we hid and watched her come outside with a puzzled look on her face as she tried to figure out how the goats' milk had disappeared.

We never did anything seriously wrong, though, and our father had no need to be a strict disciplinarian.

In Ciechanow, I knew of only one synagogue and it was strictly orthodox. On Sabbath, my brothers and I accompanied my father to the synagogue and participated in the services. I looked forward to going to synagogue each week because of the mysterious and spiritual feeling of the services. I didn't always understand the meanings of the various prayers and rituals, but I knew they were important to my father and so they were also important to me. I also enjoyed going to the synagogue because it was a special time to be with my father, brothers, uncles and other male members of my family while we practiced our religion.

At the age of thirteen, the religious community recognized me when I studied for, and completed the Bar Mitzvah ceremony. Each of my older brothers had completed the same ceremony when they reached the age of thirteen.

As Jews, we understood that the non-Jewish population of Ciechanow considered us different. Besides our synagogue, the only other religious establishment in Ciechanow that I knew about was the Catholic Church located on a hill overlooking the town.

The priest, who had been assigned to that church for many years, was a very powerful force in the community. He lived some eight to ten miles outside the city on an estate.

Although we sometimes associated with non-Jews, did business with them, and played sports with them, the one thing we never did was enter non-Jewish places of worship.

There was a gap between the Catholic community and us. We did business with them, but we didn't associate socially.

They lived their lives and we lived ours without conflict.

We never dreamed that our entire family, all our friends and, indeed, all Jews throughout Europe, would be targeted for elimination simply because of our faith.

Education

In those days, Ciechanow wasn't divided into sections for Jews and non-Jews. Nevertheless, most of the Jews chose to live in the area near the synagogue, the Hebrew schools, the kosher markets and so forth.

And the Jewish and Christian children attended separate public schools because of the different Sabbath observances. Jewish children went to school from Sunday through Friday and observed the Sabbath on Saturday while the Christian children attended school from Monday through Saturday and kept their Sabbath on Sunday. No one attended school in the summer.

My parents believed in the importance of a good education both from a secular and religious perspective. They felt that education was the key to a successful future, so they made sure we all went to school and studied hard.

I entered first grade when I was seven years old and graduated from seventh grade when I was thirteen. This was the end of my formal education because the local high school charged tuition and my parents could not afford to pay it. My brothers only went through sixth grade and then went to work with my father in his business.

In those days there were no school buses, so we walked several miles to school carrying our books and school supplies with us. We wore school uniforms of blue blazers and caps with shiny brims; the Polish schoolchildren wore very similar uniforms.

Occasionally, groups of Jewish and Catholic students got into intentional confrontations with shoving matches and name-calling. No one ever got seriously hurt, but we knew there were some hard feelings on both sides and we always expected a little skirmish when we met.

At the teacher level, at least for awhile, things were different. Some of our teachers were Jewish but many were Christian. I don't know if there were any Jewish teachers at the Christian school, but there may have been, especially prior to the Nazi occupation.

Our public school teachers were very strict and demanded excellence. Homework assignments and reading required several hours of study each evening. We were required to do our written homework with pen and ink so that a mistake, and our correction, would be noticed when the teacher checked it the next day. If our homework assignments did not meet the teacher's strict standards, we had to repeat the assignments until they were correct.

My favorite subjects were mathematics and geography, and I managed to get excellent grades in both. My math education came in handy while working in the concentration camp warehouse and later during my successful business career.

On a typical school day we would wake up early and one of us would run down the street to the bakery and return with a six- to eight-pound loaf of bread for breakfast. We then helped with the chores, while mother made our usual breakfast of cooked cereal, bread, butter and cheese, and a coffee-like beverage made of chicory.

After breakfast, we walked to school.

Four days a week, after finishing my last class at public school around two o'clock, I walked to Hebrew school for two and a half hours of instruction in the Jewish religion. The Hebrew teachers were learned Jews who taught their lessons in Yiddish and Hebrew. They were strict and demanded that we learn our lessons well. I went to Hebrew school for more than four years.

To this day I can still read the Hebrew language.

Friends

My earliest friends were two Christian boys whose mother was a widow. I was about seven years old at the time and don't remember their names. Although we went to different public schools the three of us ran around and played together after school.

We would play soccer in the streets or get a heavy limb from a tree to make a bat for our baseball games in a nearby field. Sometimes we'd take off across the bridge and head for the castle ruins on the hill just outside of town where we'd wander around and play imaginary games.

We were too young then for prejudice, and our times together were good. But as we became older, we grew apart and eventually had nothing more to do with each other.

This was typical of many relationships between Jews and non-Jews in those days, not only in Ciechanow, but most likely throughout the rest of Eastern Europe.

Over the years, my family developed long-standing friendships with several Christian families in our neighborhood. During the Christmas holidays we were invited to their homes to share cookies and other holiday treats. We always visited them on the second day of Christmas since we Jews considered it bad luck to visit a Christian family on the first day of Christmas.

As our family grew, my mother hired a Polish Catholic woman, Miss Viercza, to help with the household. She worked in our home a few days a week for several years.

My two little sisters loved and respected this kind and gentle woman. Once a year, Miss Viercza went on a pilgrimage to the Catholic shrine at Czestochowa. We knew she walked most of the way and that she would be gone for several months. During those periods, we really missed her and couldn't wait for her to return. After the first day of the Nazi occupation, we never saw or heard from her again.

My mother also was very friendly with a kind, well-to-do, Christian lady named Mrs. Wesolowski. Her family owned the largest Polish ham and sausage factory in the area and also owned the first apartment building where my family lived.

During the Passover and Easter holidays, she sent cakes and cookies to our family, and my mother reciprocated by sending matzo to her. Although the two women developed a close and trusting friendship, they always met secretly because they feared that the woman's Polish friends would ostracize her for being friendly with a Jew.

Our apartment overlooked Mrs. Wesolowski's very large garden, and at times, she shared her fresh vegetables, honey and flowers with my mother. Occasionally, she even loaned money to my mother who, being a proud and honorable person, always repaid the loan as soon as possible.

Even without modern conveniences, our home was always clean and supplied with ample food.

When I was a little boy, my older brothers often brought their friends home after work where they'd sit and talk about what was going on in their lives.

My mother welcomed them into our home and always managed to have homemade treats to feed them. In the summertime she made blueberry turnovers and other pastries and goodies. There were lots of fruits — strawberries, sour cherries, currants and gooseberries — and in the spring she served up rhubarb cooked with lots of sugar to sweeten its tangy, green-apple flavor.

One of my brother's friends always liked to tease me. He would sit at the table telling frightening tales while I stood by wide-eyed and mesmerized.

"Angel of Death," my mother would call him, in her scolding Yiddish. But even though she got upset over those stories, she always encouraged my brothers and me to bring our friends home.

Our home was a busy, happy place overflowing with family and friends. Many nights, after the evening meal, my uncles and aunts would come to visit. While we cousins played, the adults would gather around the big table in the kitchen to talk. They would tell stories, often they would sing. But what I remember most as a child was the cadence of their voices and their laughter as it rang out into the night.

Daily Life in Ciechanow

Even though we didn't live in poverty, we didn't live an easy life either. Our family was considered by our neighbors and friends to be respectable and honorable, and the family business was a success.

All of us — my father, my mother, four brothers, two sisters and I — always had to work hard. The children wore hand-me-down clothes, and we all did chores willingly. We never complained about the hard work and second-hand clothes; that's just the way life was.

Life in our part of Eastern Europe was more primitive than in the west. Running water and indoor plumbing was out of the question, but we did have electricity, and even with our tight quarters, there was always a place to do our homework.

Life was the same everywhere.

The streets outside our apartment were paved with cobblestones and kept swept clean by the tenants in the buildings that lined each side. Traffic consisted of horses and buggies since the town had only one passenger car, owned by the druggist. We had trucks for the family poultry business, but they were driven by helpers hired by my father and were never used for our personal transportation.

Our apartment was on the ground floor of a brick, four-story building that was occupied by thirty or more Jewish families. The Catholics didn't consider the building good enough for them, but that didn't bother us because we were grateful just to have a decent place to live.

It's amazing that despite the social separation, my father did business with many Catholic farmers, and mutual respect was always shown in many ways.

Our three-room apartment — a kitchen, a parlor and bedroom — became very crowded when the entire family was present. Two of my brothers often slept at my aunt's home, which gave the rest of us a little more space. As I look back on those days, I wonder how we all managed to live in harmony in such crowded conditions. I guess it's because we loved each other and got along well.

And, we had the occasional escape to my father's poultry farm just outside of town. We'd hitch the horse to the wagon and ride out to the farm with father where we'd help him with the poultry or just wander through the countryside. We loved being out in nature, loved watching the birds and loved playing in the forests and fields. We also loved spending time with the family dog that lived at the farm most of the time, except when father gave into our begging and allowed him to come back to town with us for a day or two.

Of course, that was in the summer. The winters were a different matter altogether.

Poland is a cold, dark land in the winter.

Luckily, the apartments where we lived stayed fairly warm all night because coal furnaces heated them. The fire in the kitchen wood stove, however, sometimes went out during the night, forcing my mother to thaw out the solid block of ice in the water barrel before she could cook breakfast and we could wash up for the day.

One of my chores each morning was to fill the water barrel. I placed a wooden yoke across my shoulders, attached two empty buckets to it and walked to the community well several miles away. I filled the buckets, attached them back on the ends of the yoke and walked back home.

Several days a week I made more than one trip to the well to get extra water for cooking, meals, bathing or laundry.

Laundry day was a major undertaking for my mother who boiled and scrubbed our linens and clothing and hung them on lines strung across the rooms. On laundry day, our small apartment was transformed into a maze that smelled of soap and humidity and rang with calls of admonition from my mother as she strove to protect her hard work from the grubby hands of seven active offspring.

We never knew the luxury of a shower, but my mother insisted that our bodies and clothing always be clean.

Poland's fertile plains in general, and the rural area around Ciechanow in particular, were blessed with very rich soil that produced abundant harvests. It was Poland's blessing and her curse. Her people have fought many wars through the centuries because first one nation then another wanted to claim her rich lands as their own.

Wheat grew tall there. Grain was plentiful. Sugar beets, which grew fat and sweet in this area, were another staple crop. After the beet harvest, the farmers loaded their wagons full to overflowing to take them to the sugar beet factory. We followed behind those wagons, and if any beets fell off, we quickly scooped them up and ran home. My mother made wonderful beet preserves that were so sweet you never had to add sugar.

Many of the streets in the city were lined with fruit trees. We weren't allowed to pick the fruit to take home, but anyone could take some to eat as they walked.

Before the Nazi occupation, my father made sure that we always had plenty to eat and my mother managed the household frugally. Whenever my mother cooked a chicken, duck or goose she rendered the fat and used it for seasoning and cooking. We sometimes spread the fat on bread and made a meal out of it. My mother also made use of the goose down and feathers in pillows and blankets. Nothing was ever wasted.

Landowners in Ciechanow had the added advantage of being able to hunt for game. After the annual grain harvest, it was traditional for the Polish landowners to hunt quail and other game on their large estates.

On several occasions, when I was about ten years old, I accompanied the owner of the sausage factory as he hunted quail in his grain fields. Before the hunt, he gave me a special belt to wear. When I retrieved the quail from the field, I would hang them on the loops of my belt so they could be carried home.

At the end of each hunt I had fifteen or twenty big fat quail hanging from my belt. He never shared those quail with me, but he always treated me very kindly during those times we spent together.

We didn't eat meat more than three times a week usually. And while we had chickens, we never ate eggs unless we were sick.

Beef was only eaten on the Sabbath.

My mother bought processed grain by the kilo and made noodles quite frequently. We had very little fried food. Most of our meals were cooked on top of the stove, meat and vegetables together. Even when we ate fish, it was cooked with the vegetables.

In those days, everyone had a garden. It wasn't enough to provide all the needs of a family such as ours, but it helped. And it was a form of recreation for my mother. She enjoyed working in the soil.

There were no supermarkets where we could buy canned or frozen vegetables, so in the fall, every family had to make sure they had enough vegetables to last through the long, cold Polish winter.

Each October, we stored large quantities of potatoes, onions, and dried mushrooms in our shed and covered them with straw to make sure they didn't freeze or rot.

We also bought hundreds of pounds of cabbage that we shredded into a fifty-gallon wooden cabbage barrel. We added salt and other ingredients that turned it into naturally fermented sauerkraut.

As children, we worked for hours shredding the cabbage with a hand-operated shredder with two steel knife blades. Hour after hour, we children took turns using the shredder and filling the fifty-gallon barrel to the brim. It was hard work but we understood that it was necessary to enable us to get through the winter in good health. After our family finished shredding the cabbage, other families in our building borrowed the shredder. Each day after school, my mother sent one of us to the shed to stir the cabbage with a large stick to allow the gasses to escape. During the winter months the fermenting sauerkraut, potatoes, onions and dried mushrooms from that shed were our only source of vegetables.

There were no refrigerators in our home or in the homes of any of our friends. During the very cold winters, men cut huge blocks of ice from the frozen rivers and lakes and stored them in a large icehouse. Wood shavings, used as insulation, kept the blocks of ice frozen until late summer. My father occasionally bought a large block of ice and used it to keep meat, cheese, and other foods cool in our basement.

Our family was very grateful that we always had enough to eat and we shared our blessings with others less fortunate.

Since the Sabbath began on Friday at sundown and work was forbidden until sundown Saturday, people prepared the Sabbath meal on Friday.

On most Friday afternoons, my uncle Leibel gathered the boys together, loaded our arms with chickens and egg breads (chala) and had us deliver them to several families in our neighborhood who were not as well off as we were. We never looked down on those people; they were just neighbors who were having a hard time. I have tried to honor Uncle Leibel's memory by following his example to this day.

The Altus Family Business

My father was a poultry and fowl dealer who operated a business that had been in our family for several generations.

Each day he went into the countryside around Ciechanow to buy geese, ducks, chickens and turkeys from farmers. He then brought them to his small farm on the outskirts of the city where they were fattened up and prepared for sale. After the birds reached the proper size and weight, he shipped most of them to Germany in special trains designed for carrying live fowl. My father shipped the rest in trucks to the marketplaces of Warsaw and other Polish cities.

Looking back, it is interesting that in spite of all the separation between Jews and Catholics, my father did business successfully with everyone.

His office was in his pocket. There, he carried a small ledger book where he recorded how many geese or other birds he got from each farm. On his next trip he paid the farmer.

This business relationship was based on the mutual respect and trust that developed between the Jewish poultry dealer and the Polish farmers even though they were from distinctly different backgrounds. Despite thousands of transactions over the years, there were never any invoices and never a dispute.

Your word was your bond.

On most days, the farmers invited my father to share the noon meal. They observed his dietary restrictions, and made sure that he didn't get any pork or other unkosher food.

On our family's farm, the birds always had a supply of fresh water and grain. It was essential that they have a heavy layer of fat before being taken to market. I can distinctly remember watching the birds stick their heads out of their stalls to eat the grain and drink the water from troughs which ran alongside. It seemed as though their entire existence was spent with their heads sticking out into the feed troughs.

One day, when I was about ten years old and school was out, my father took me along with one of his helpers on a buying trip. One farmer had a large flock of 150 to 200 geese to sell, so my father asked his helper to walk them directly back the eight or nine miles to our small farm.

After the goose herder left with the flock, my father and I went to another farm. Unexpectedly, that farmer also had a large flock to sell. By that time, the goose herder was too far ahead for me to catch up to him with the second flock.

It looked as though my father would have to pass up the purchase until I spoke up.

I saw a chance to do something important and asked permission to walk the geese to our farm alone. By this time it was three or four o'clock in the afternoon. Geese walk slowly, and the distance to our farm was far. My father must have seen how much it meant to me, because he reluctantly agreed. He turned his horse and buggy toward town, and I set off down the road with about 100 geese under my questionable control.

 I adored my father and would not fail him under any circumstances. I was proud that he had given me an adult's job, and I knew the geese were a big financial responsibility. I realized that the behavior of a large flock of geese was very unpredictable and that they might scatter if anything spooked them, so I stayed busy keeping them together as we walked through the forest and villages on the way to our farm.

In the middle of the night, I saw a stranger sitting alone at the edge of the forest. As I approached him, I asked what time it was, keeping a wary eye on him as I moved the geese down the path. I was very relieved that he didn't bother me or try to steal any of the geese.

As night turned into morning, I approached the pond near our farm and feared once again that I might lose the geese if they decided to scatter and run into the water. As I looked into the distance, I was pleased to see my father with his horse and buggy coming to meet me.

To this day, that long overnight walk through the dark forest remains the most frightening thing I ever did as a child. Although I remember being very scared, there was no way I was going to disappoint my father by losing even one of those geese.

When I arrived home that morning I found that my mother was very upset with my father for allowing me to walk all night alone. We couldn't know then that my father would not live to guide me to manhood. However, by giving me that responsibility as a young boy, he left me with one of my most treasured memories.

At Christmas time, a turkey dinner was traditional in Polish homes. Chickens were never in demand during the holidays. My father always provided fat turkeys as holiday gifts to the mayor of Ciechanow and to other city officials, including the chief of police. It became my job to deliver those live turkeys and I remember receiving some very large tips from the police chief.

Our family business owned a few trucks with which we shipped live fowl to Warsaw. The first trip I took out of Ciechanow was on a poultry truck that was going to deliver a load of live geese to the Warsaw marketplace. Even though we were only a relatively short distance from Warsaw, the trip seemed to take hours. When we got to the big city we made the delivery and then immediately headed back to Ciechanow. I was very disappointed that I didn't have a chance to look around and see the sights. I think I was about ten years old when I took that trip. Although I made other trips to Warsaw before the war, I never did get a chance to just be a tourist.

My Uncle Leibel, my mother's brother, was a grain broker. Unlike like my father, who dealt primarily with the owners of smaller farms, Uncle Leibel's business dealings were mainly with the owners of the large estate farms outside the city. Before the harvest season, while the grain was still in the field, he and the estate owners agreed on a price for grain.

Uncle Leibel bought grain contracts on speculation, similar to today's commodity market. After the harvest, he moved the grain into large storage areas from which it was later sold to other businesses. Uncle Leibel employed several men to keep turning the grain in the storage silos to prevent it from rotting and combusting.

One of his best customers for grain was the owner of Ciechanow's large brewery. Each Saturday, Uncle Leibel sent me and one of my brothers to the brewery to get a case of beer, which was provided free to him. In those days, beer came in bottles with corks. Occasionally, my brother and I popped a cork out of a bottle and drank some beer on the way home. Uncle Leibel probably knew what we had done, but he never reported us to our parents.

While Uncle Leibel dealt in much larger contracts than my father did, he conducted his business in the same ethical way. They both kept accurate records and worked on their honor.

The price of grain fluctuated then just like it does now. Sometimes he discussed his business dealings with my mother in the evenings. He was a very wealthy man before the Nazis confiscated his business, and to this day no one has made restitution for what was stolen from him and my father.

As a boy, I remember my father telling my brothers and me about the incidents where some priests and other influential men preached hatred towards the Jews. It was designed to cause the Polish population to hate us. Nevertheless, life for a Jewish boy growing up in Ciechanow, Poland, during the late 1920s and early 1930s, was very secure and safe.

My parents provided guidance and love. My brothers, sisters, uncles, aunts and cousins gave me a strong sense of the importance of family.

My teachers in public school and Hebrew school demanded excellence and instilled a strong desire for knowledge.

My friends and playmates provided hours of fun and companionship.

It was a sweet, wonderful existence for us all.

Never in any of our wildest imaginations could we have predicted the horror and tragedy that soon awaited us.

PART TWO

THE INVASION

The Nazi Occupation Begins

By the late 1930s, it became apparent that something bad was about to happen in Poland. There was clearly a change in the relationships between the German residents of Poland (the Volksdeutsche) and the rest of the population. The organized preaching against Jews had taken hold in the non-Jewish society.

I don't remember if we had access to newspapers, but the people in our community, in spite of their simple living conditions, somehow managed to stay informed and to exchange ideas.

Hardly anyone owned a radio. At that time, they were 100 times more rare than home computers are now. But one of our friends had one, and he would place it on the windowsill of his home and turn its speaker to face the street. We were close enough to the Prussian border that we received very clear radio signals, and what we heard, chilled us to the core.

I was maybe thirteen years old when I first became aware that life was changing. I was very mature, more so than thirteen-year-olds today. I had finished school and had been apprenticed to a furniture maker.

I was standing in the street with a small group of my neighbors, and we were listening to Hitler's screaming tirades. No one made a sound. In stunned silence, we listened, shivering in the warm sunshine, as the voice of a madman rang out so clear it was as if he were in the street right behind us.

Hitler had cast his shadow over Ciechanow and we were powerless to dispel it.

Between 1938 and 1939 everything in Ciechanow came to a standstill.

Gradually, so very gradually, life as we knew it began to shut down. People were so uncertain and anxious about the future that nobody did any planning. Businesses began to close, and families drew close together. When the summer of 1938 ended, the schools never reopened.

By the beginning of 1939, the Volksdeutsche began organizing boycotts and marches against Jewish businesses. Their mission was to incite the Polish population against the Jews, and they were very successful in doing so. It was clear to us that the very powerful anti-Jewish movement taking place throughout Poland had the wholehearted support of most of the Polish population.

Soon, it seemed all the non-Jewish people had turned against us. They marched in front of our businesses. They spit on us in the streets. We became angry and fearful, but what could we do? There was no answer for it. We kept to ourselves and tried to ignore it.

Life grew increasingly difficult and depressing. as psychologically the Jewish community began to break down.

It was impossible to know then, however, that we were soon to experience the absolute evil of concentration camps, beatings, torture, mass executions and the systematic elimination of most of Europe's Jews.

That year, many German Jewish families, thinking they were escaping the Nazis, crossed the East Prussian border into Poland and settled in and around the city of Ciechanow. My family and other Jewish residents helped them find places to live and provided food and other necessities of daily living. We certainly never realize that none of us was destined to remain in Ciechanow much longer.

During that period, most Jews had no idea that the Nazis would soon target them for extermination. Even those who could imagine it simply did not have the means or opportunity to escape from Europe.

Where were we to go? Ciechanow had been our haven for generations. This was home. It was where you were safe.

We feared the Russians nearly as much as the Germans, so fleeing to the East was out of the question. To our south were Slovakia, Hungary and Romania, all of which were in as much peril as we were in Poland. To our north were Prussia, Lithuania and the Baltic Sea. There was nowhere to run nowhere to hide. The feeling was like being in a cage with no hope of ever being free. The feeling of hopelessness was almost overwhelming, especially for the adults and older teenagers in the Jewish community.

Of course, the non-Jewish people seemed to go about their daily lives as they always had done, but they were not without fear. The Poles themselves were increasingly concerned about their own welfare.

They knew their history of past invasions, of ancestors caught between warring nations that wanted to claim Poland's ample harvests for food and her strong people for free labor. They had heard the rumors that Poland was next on Hitler's list of lands to conquer.

And they had heard it would come the next fall, after the grain was harvested for winter.

They were right.

Early on the afternoon of September 1, 1939, the expected Nazi occupation of Poland began.

I was on the sidewalk outside our family's apartment that afternoon when I first heard the roar of aircraft engines. I looked up into the blue autumn sky and saw the source – German planes flying low over the city.

I ducked back inside our apartment building as the bullets smashed into windows and shells exploded in the streets. The train station was destroyed. Homes, apartments, stores and businesses were reduced to ruin. Although the air attack was brief, the damage throughout the city was extensive.

It was clear that the German pilots were intentionally targeting the civilian population. We cowered in our apartment and were among the lucky ones for the moment. There were bullet holes all over our building, but our apartment itself received little damage, and no one was hurt.

No armies marched into town that day. No heavy artillery moved on its streets, but we knew the invasion we feared had begun.

The day after our city was bombed and strafed, my father gathered our family together, loaded a few belongings onto his horse and buggy and moved us to the town of Nowe Miasto (Neustadt), a short distance south of Ciechanow. It was farther from the Prussian border, and he thought it would be farther away from the immediate impact of the invasion. No one stopped us or bothered us while we were traveling, and we remained in Nowe Miasto with family friends for a few days until my father determined that it was safe enough to return to our home in Ciechanow.

My brother, Yussel, brought his bicycle to Nowe Miasto. He was riding it behind the buggy on the way back to Ciechanow when I spotted a German army patrol approaching on bicycles. I knew they would confiscate my brother's bike if they saw him, so I quickly called him over and let the air out of his tires. I hoisted the bike onto my shoulder, hoping they would think it was useless.

When the German bike patrol came up to us they looked at the bicycle and us. Seeing the flat tires, they moved on and didn't bother us. It was the first, but definitely not the last time that I outwitted the Nazis during the next six years.

Back in Ciechanow, German troops wearing Wehrmacht uniforms had already occupied the city. The Polish Army was no match for them, especially with the city's native Germans collaborating with the invaders. We knew we had Nazi sympathizers living in our community, but we never knew their activities were so organized until we saw them in action after the invasion had taken place. The "Kristallnacht" violence had already occurred in Germany, and it had spilled over into a boycott of Jewish businesses in Poland. The Nazis met no effective opposition in Poland and accomplished their takeover quickly and efficiently.

German officers immediately confiscated the nicest homes and apartments throughout the city and eventually brought their families there to live with them.

When we returned to Ciechanow, my father learned that his poultry business and my Uncle Leibel's grain business had been confiscated. This was told to him discretely, secretly. People were watching, and no assembly or discussion of any kind was allowed.

My family was never reimbursed in any way for the assets that the Nazi's stole from them. I have no idea whether the Nazi's continued to operate those businesses, as they did with the Polish farms they confiscated, or whether they simply used up all the assets and moved on. Of course, after the businesses were confiscated, we never went near them again. After many generations as self-sufficient, hard-workers the Altus family no longer had any means of income. Our psychological and physical existence became more difficult with each passing day.

We had no idea at the time that our living conditions would continue to get much worse.

Jewish-owned businesses were not the only ones affected by the Nazi takeover. Polish businesses, industries and farms also were confiscated. The Nazis forced the large estate farmers to remain on their farms and manage them for their new Nazi "owners." The entire product of the

Polish nation was now firmly under the Nazis' direct control.

Daily life for the Jewish community of Ciechanow quickly deteriorated. The Volksdeutsche, who had been joyfully anticipating the arrival of the Nazis, put on their swastika armbands and told the Nazis where all the Jews were living. The Nazis immediately rounded-up groups of Jews and sent them out daily on forced-labor details. The Nazis ordered a curfew from sundown to sunup that restricted all occupants of the city, Jews and Poles alike, to their homes. The Nazis forbade the population to assemble and to worship. The synagogue, the church and schools were immediately closed.

Within a few months, the SS and Gestapo arrived in Ciechanow to supplement the regular German army troops. They made their presence known to us by quickly implementing more brutal control measures on the citizens, especially on the Jewish population. With the arrival of the SS and Gestapo, the Jews of Ciechanow became even more afraid of what the future held in store for them.

The atrocities started slowly, but after a few months of occupation, they became commonplace and expected. Signs were posted everywhere denouncing Jews. All Jews were required to wear yellow Stars of David on their clothing. This identified us to the rest of the population. Jewish males were required to shave their beards and mustaches. The Nazis forbade Jews to use sidewalks and ordered us to walk in the gutters. If a Jew was seen walking on a sidewalk he would be kicked, beaten and spit upon not only by the Nazis, but also by his former neighbors and friends.

Young terrorists belonging to the Hitler Youth organization randomly stormed into Jewish homes at night and committed vicious acts of violence, destruction and terror. They beat, tortured and intimidated Jews throughout the city. The Nazis declared "open season" on the entire Jewish community, and there were no limits on the amount or type of physical and psychological terror inflicted on them by the Nazis and their sympathizers. Never was an SS, Gestapo, Nazi, or sympathizer held accountable for any atrocity done to a Jew. On the other hand, they were encouraged to kill, beat, torture, or abuse Jews simply because of their religion.

Although I never personally witnessed it, there were many stories of Hitler Youth forcing Jewish men and boys to watch the Nazis rape their wives, mothers and sisters. They even broke into homes and forced brothers and sisters to have sexual intercourse while they watched.

They never looked at us as fellow human beings, rather we were considered to be something less than human in their eyes. While I know that the above atrocities happened frequently, I refrain from talking about them when I visit schools to discuss the Holocaust with children. I thought during those long months of the Nazi occupation that I would never again see anything as cruel as what the Nazis did to us in Ciechanow simply because we were Jews.

But I was so very wrong.

Winter set in in October that year, bringing with it sub-zero temperatures and heavy, wet snows.

Early each morning the Nazis rounded up hundreds of young Jewish men and women from their homes and took them out to perform forced labor. Those who were unable to keep up with the fast pace set by the Nazis were severely beaten.

Some days we worked cleaning and repairing the homes and buildings that the Nazis confiscated and now occupied.

When the snows came, they forced us, in below-freezing temperatures, to clean it off the streets and sidewalks. Of course, it was all right for us to walk on the sidewalks as long as we were shoveling and sweeping the snow away, but not at any other time.

Normally we got no food during the workday. One day, my mother gave me a bread roll that I put in my pocket before going out to work. When I took the roll out of my pocket for lunch, I found it had frozen solid. My fingers became frostbitten, but from morning to night, day after endless day, we shoveled snow.

One day, my father came home injured and bleeding from a beating he had received at the hands of the Nazis. He wasn't sure what he had done wrong because they never told us anything. They pushed, shoved and cursed us, calling us names and screaming in our ears. But they never explained anything. Never.

My mother tended his injuries in silence, and we never talked about what had happened. The walls had ears, and we could take no chances.

We had lost so much from our normal life. Not only were we short of food, but none of us had extra clothes. Each morning we put on the same damp clothing we had worn the day before. By the time we reached our work sites we were once again soaked from trudging through the wet snow. Every day we suffered from cold, hunger, thirst and fatigue.

But it wasn't the hunger and other physical agonies that destroyed us. It was the psychological tortures that drove us to despair. Everything they did was designed to bring our morale down to zero.

They had a very clever way of breaking you down. If one person resisted, they would shoot many. You couldn't even have a facial expression of dissatisfaction. You had to be stone-faced, stoic. You had to be made of steel.

They stole our homes, our businesses, our livelihoods. They took away all our means of self-care and preservation.

They strove to destroy our faith.

The Germans reached a new level of hatred when they turned our synagogue into a garage.

Before the occupation, no one ever drove to synagogue. We did not work on the Sabbath, so the men of the community would walk to worship. The temple itself sat back off the street, a long wide walkway running from its large entranceway to the road where we walked.

It was a place of great sacredness, which the Germans detested, and seeking to hurt us all at the deepest level they knew how, they turned our most holy gathering place into a home for their machines of war. They fouled the air with their diesel fumes and profanities. They spilled grease and oil upon the floors and looted our religious relics.

Then, in their most profane gesture, they rolled our treasured Torahs out on the ground and allowed their military trucks and other vehicles to run over them, desecrating the most sacred symbols of our religion.

One night, five Jewish elders embarked on a daring plan to protect the remaining Torahs from desecration until the war was over. They crept into the synagogue, removed several Torahs, and buried them in the Jewish cemetery. However, the Polish caretaker of the cemetery happened to see them and informed the Nazis.

Early in 1942, the Nazis rounded up the five men, elders Mlozker, Golozer, Rumianek, Savek and Tiblum. The Nazis then forced the entire Jewish population to come to the city square and watch in anguished silence as the Nazis hanged the heroic elders.

After the hanging, there was nothing to say. We never spoke of it, not even in the privacy of our own homes. There was no way to ease the horror for the children. We could only hold them close and try to quiet their frightened sobs.

For ourselves, we lived with the terror and pain in solitude and learned not to let it show, not to let it own us. It is like getting physically beaten. The first few blows really hurt. After that, you get numb.

During the high holidays, however, we risked death by assembling in the fourth floor attic of our apartment building for religious services.

Every crevice and crack was covered so no trace of candlelight would escape. Our prayers were sung in whispers, but our faith would not be denied.

Several people stood watch outside and in apartment windows. If German soldiers, Volksdeutsche or Hitler Youth approached our building, the lookouts signaled a warning. If we had been caught praying, the Nazis would have shot us on the spot.

Even though we had to cease observing the Jewish rituals and traditions, my father still managed not to eat anything that was not kosher because he deeply believed in the teachings of our faith.

One of the most important kosher rules required that animals be slaughtered according to a strict ritual. In our community there was a special building where the animals were killed by the "Shohet," the person responsible for complying with the kosher rituals. According to rules of kosher, the knife used for slaughter had to be razor sharp without any nicks on the blade. Any blade with imperfections had to be thrown away. Literally, Shohet means "they feel no pain."

There was nothing mysterious about the kosher requirements. They were designed to ensure that Jews consumed food that met the purity standards prescribed by our religion. Nevertheless, before the occupation the Polish government tried to outlaw kosher killing.

After the invasion, the Shohet was in constant danger because he refused to stop what he believed God had called him to do. When kosher food preparation became a forbidden act, a young Catholic woman named Yanka carried the ritual knives for the Shohet until it was safe for him to use them.

Yanka worked for many years for one of my uncles in his ladies' designer clothing business. She spoke Yiddish fluently and was very friendly with our family despite the prejudices the rest of her community held against us. By doing this selfless act for the Shohet, and for all of us in the Jewish community, she risked her life. I never knew what happened to her.

As the Nazi occupation continued, atrocities worsened. My father was required to shave his mustache and wear the Star of David. He sometimes came home bruised and bleeding after having been kicked and beaten by non-Jews, some of whom he knew well and once counted among his friends. It was incomprehensible to me how a well-respected person such as my father could become a victim of such blind hatred, and yet he had. We all had.

One of the most agonizing ways this hatred was made manifest to us every day was in the disappearance of our friends and loved ones. We secretly prayed every morning when we left our homes and families that we would all be together again at the end of the day.

These were no idle prayers. Our numbers were dwindling and we were left to grieve and wonder without hope of ever knowing what had happened to those we loved.

One day, my brother Leibel went out on his daily work detail and didn't come back. We never saw him again.

One of my female cousins disappeared the same way. Her father, my mother's brother, survived the Holocaust and later died in New York.

We mourned them then.

We mourn them still.

A Jewish Hero

In the fall of 1941, the Nazis rounded up as many as 200 young, healthy Jewish women and sent them out to the large estate farms to harvest the potato crop. Those farms, which the Nazis previously confiscated, were now being managed by their former owners under direct Nazi control.

The Nazis demanded that the farms maximize their production in order to contribute to the war effort. Unlike the men and boys working on the roads, the young women stayed overnight on the farms. They were required to dig potatoes by hand from morning to night under the most brutal working conditions.

The farm managers provided little or no shelter, food or tools. In general, the Nazis treated those women worse than farm animals.

My uncle, Leibel Altus, was a wonderful man who demonstrated love and kindness towards his family, and care and concern for those less fortunate than himself.

His family always came first, his business came second, and his deep love of horses came third. He raised and rode show horses, which he kept on the outskirts of Ciechanow.

Over the years, Uncle Leibel had built up a very good working relationship with those Poles who were now being forced to manage the farms they had previously owned. He had bought their grain crops for many years, and they knew that he was an honest, reliable businessman.

Uncle Leibel decided it might be worthwhile to try to talk them into improving conditions for the young women forced to work there.

He was not expecting to accomplish much because he knew the Nazis would not stand for it, but he thought it would be worth a try.

Uncle Leibel still had one of the horses he had owned before the occupation. One day, he saddled up and rode into the countryside to see what he could do. He rode from farm to farm asking the managers to do anything they could to give the young women more food, shelter and tools. Any improvement would be welcome, he surmised.

He knew he was taking a serious risk, but he refused to just sit back and allow those young women to continue to be treated so poorly.

It just wasn't in his character to do such a thing if there were any hope at all that his influence could make some difference.

Uncle Leibel's own four children, two girls and two boys, were too young to be taken to the work details, but he wanted none of those young people to suffer if he could affect even the smallest change.

Apparently someone, maybe even one of his former friends, tipped off the Nazis about his so-called subversive activities.

One day, after again riding out to the farms, he failed to return home. After losing my brother Leibel and a cousin, our family feared the worst. Several days later we heard the news.

The local police who patrolled the roads had seized him, probably on some Nazi's order.

They then took him into the woods and shot him to death.

PART THREE

AUSCHWITZ-BIRKENAU

Transport to Auschwitz-Birkenau

As the occupation progressed, the Nazis continued to appropriate houses and apartments, confining the Jewish community into a smaller and smaller section of the city. By this time we had four families crowded into our tiny three-room apartment.

We slept on the floor. We had no coal for the furnace, so we tore down wooden fences and burned them for heat. Everyone struggled and shared. The occupation had been going on for three years, and nothing shocked us anymore.

During the latter part of October 1942, the Nazis notified some of the Jewish leaders in our community that they intended to relocate the entire Jewish population of Ciechanow.

The way the Nazis communicated with us was to give our leaders information to relay. It was easy for the leaders to reach all of us by then, because everyone was crowded into such a small area.

The Jewish leaders spoke very carefully. They could not publicly encourage or organize any opposition to the Nazis because there were informers and collaborators hidden everywhere who might overhear and report this information to the Nazis. Anyone who attracted the attention of a soldier or informer risked beating or death for himself and his family.

We were told to report to the train station on a certain day. We were to wear our best clothing and take our two most precious belongings with us.

When I found out that we were going to be resettled in a new area where we could live and work, I was relieved. Our day-to-day existence in Ciechanow was unbearable. I had become a man during the occupation. At age eighteen, I believed I knew a bit about the world, and while I certainly didn't trust the Nazis, I hoped that a move to a new area would offer a chance at a new beginning for all of us.

One of our family's friends, the city blacksmith, had relatives in the United States. The Nazis had allowed him to keep his shop open so they could force him to work for them.

A day or two before we were to leave, I stopped by the blacksmith shop to see how he and his family was doing and to learn how he felt about the relocation.

When I walked into the shop, however, I couldn't believe my eyes. He was standing before the blazing furnace, and one by one, he was tossing American hundred dollar bills into the billowing fire.

"They might get me," he said in answer to my astonished questioning, "but they'll never get my money."

Those words left me reeling.

I was devastated.

In that instant I finally faced what I had not wanted to believe. I suddenly realized what the future held in store for us. My hopes of a new beginning were shattered.

I never saw the blacksmith again.

On the appointed morning, my father and mother gathered the family and made sure we were dressed in our best clothes. My mother had decided which of our possessions to take, and we dutifully held tight to our "treasures" and walked as a family down the street.

My father was fifty years old, and my mother was forty-eight. My brother Yussel was twenty-seven, Srulek was twenty-five, Simon was twenty-three, my sister Chaia was fourteen and Feigel was eleven. I was eighteen years old. Leibel, who had been taken away by the Nazis more than a year earlier, would have been twenty.

As we walked towards the train station, aunts, uncles, cousins, friends and neighbors joined us.

The entire remaining Jewish community of Ciechanow, dressed in our best clothing and carrying our most prized possessions, walked slowly and solemnly to the trains, which were about to carry us into hell on earth.

As I walked with them and watched them, I was overcome by feelings of sadness, fear, anger and loathing.

Primary was the heartbreak of leaving our homes and all we had known and loved about our once-fair city of Ciechanow. But there also was the fear of what lay ahead and the unbelievable anger and loathing I felt towards those absolutely evil persons who were causing this to happen.

To our surprise, the Nazis conducted the roundup in a quiet, orderly manner. No force was used. There were no beatings, no shouts or rage or derision.

We were treated so uncharacteristically well while moving onto the train that many grew to feel a false sense of optimism. I now suspect the Nazis treated us well as a way to keep us off guard and prevent any defiance or resistance on that crucial day. They didn't want any scenes, and it was no problem for them to camouflage things. They were in complete control.

Even those among us who doubted that we were going to a better life would not endanger their families by resisting.

The train that transported us was a relatively comfortable passenger train, unlike the cattle-car trains on which most of the Jews were transported to the death camps.

We were on that train for several days, during which time it moved sporadically through the countryside. Often it stopped for hours and we just watched and waited.

We were grateful for the few bites of roll and bits of cheese my mother had packed to stave off the hunger, since she rightly guessed that no one would bother to feed us. Of course, after three years of the occupation, we were not accustomed to eating much.

Although we were concerned about what our final destination was to be, we were not overly worried about it. We realized there was nothing we could do to change our lot. Our fate was in the hands of the Nazis, and while we knew they were brutal and malicious, we still had some vague, unrealistic hope that they really intended to resettle us and allow us to resume our way of life.

Then, very late on the night of Saturday, November 7, 1942, our train started to slow down.

Looking out the windows, we saw a huge area surrounded by bright lights. It appeared to be deserted. Nothing moved.

The lights were so bright there, you could have comfortably read a book by them, although it was in the middle of a moonless night.

As the train came to a complete stop, there was absolute silence. No one spoke. No one moved.

We just stared out the windows.

Suddenly, the train door was yanked open from outside and there, silhouetted against the light, were SS soldiers with vicious guard dogs that lunged against their leashes, snarling and snapping at the stunned people inside.

We did not know it then, but we were inside the Birkenau section of the infamous Auschwitz concentration camp complex.

We had entered the gates of hell.

Selection

No one spoke a word.

The guards ordered us off the train, pushed us roughly and shoved us into long lines on the platform. They marched us towards an SS officer who glanced at each person then gestured with his thumb sending the men and older boys in one direction, and the younger women in another.

The elderly and women with young children were sent straight ahead. We later found out that this was "selection," the process by which the Nazis separated those who could work from those who could not.

At first we didn't know what was happening. By the time we realized that they were dividing us up, it was too late for good-byes.

I watched the Nazis march my mother, my sisters, Chaia and Feigel, my aunts, and other female cousins and friends away. Everything was quiet. It was impossible for my mother to speak or even wave goodbye to me or me to her.

My eyes filled with tears, and I watched them move slowly into the distance until they disappeared from my sight into the dark of the night.

I never saw them again.

The Nazis marched my group of men and older boys into a building where they handed each of us a piece of paper with a number on it. They pushed us over to a table where I gave the paper to a prisoner who immediately tattooed number 73538 on my left forearm. It remains there to this day.

The tattoo hurt a little, but I don't remember it in particular, possibly because everything else hurt. The guards shaved our heads with clippers. When they wanted me to lower my head, they hit it with the clipper. They clipped it fast and roughly, gouging out chunks of skin along with the hair. They stripped us of our clothing and gave us striped prison uniforms. Later they ran out of uniforms.

I also got a pair of dried-up old shoes. Those old shoes cut into my feet so badly that I still have the scars today.

Thinking about it today, I can still see those bright lights, those vicious guards and those snarling dogs in my mind's eye. No one had heard anything about the concentration camps, not in Ciechanow. In the bigger cities they heard more, knew more.

But hearing and seeing it with your own eyes were two very different things. No one even imagined the horror we would face. They were worse than anyone's worse nightmares.

What puzzles me is why they let any of us live to tell the story of the evil they perpetrated against us. They didn't need the workers; they had forced laborers from all over Europe. It was purely an extermination, with the forced labor thrown in as just a means to keep us busy until they could see us die.

Our group was marched to Barrack No. 9 in the main camp of Birkenau. I was stunned to numbness; my mind was a blank. I don't remember anything at all of the march to the barrack.

When we got there, we were greeted by the "barrack oldest," the prisoner who had been assigned there for the longest time. He was a veteran of the Nazi concentration camp system and knew what we had to do to survive.

I looked at my new "home" with terror and despair. More than 500 men were crammed into Barrack No. 9, a converted wooden building that had once been a horse stable. Three tiers of "bunks" — nothing more than wooden shelves — filled the long structure, with each bunk containing a thin sack of straw that served as a poor excuse for a mattress.

The "barrack oldest" assigned me to a bunk pallet with four other prisoners. My place was on the top row, the third layer from the bottom. Even lying shoulder to shoulder, five of us would not fit on the bunk. The space was less than six feet wide. None of us could even lie flat.

They issued each of us a thin dark gray blanket that did not begin to keep out the bitter cold. We had no underwear and no socks, just the cotton uniforms.

The "barrack oldest" told us we must remain on our bunks unless we were going on a work detail or some other authorized activity. The Nazis forbade us to walk around the barracks or talk with the other prisoners.

There was not much sleep in Barrack No. 9 that night. Early the next morning, which was Sunday, someone woke us by banging on the bunks. He told us to form up outside the barrack to be counted.

Of course, we had slept in our clothes since we had nothing other than the uniforms. There were no facilities for washing, so we assembled outside in a formation composed of rows of five men each. The SS guards made sure they accounted for all prisoners. Later we discovered that if there were any discrepancies in the headcount the SS guards would force us to stand there until the numbers came out right, even if it took all day.

After the SS guards counted us in the morning, they gave us a single enamel bowl containing a small amount of artificial tea, which the five prisoners in my group had to share. There was no food or anything else to drink during the rest of the day.

In the evening, we each received a small piece of bread and a tiny bowl of thin soup, mostly water with only very small pieces of potato and cabbage thrown in.

On Sunday we did not have to go to work, so we went straight back into the barrack after being counted. The only place we were allowed to go was back to our bunks. I still did not know where they sent my father or brothers, and did not know where my mother and sisters were.

I didn't go to my bunk right away. I stood in the doorway looking out at the rows and rows of barracks before me. After awhile, I noticed an older prisoner nearby. He was wearing a white jacket, and since the number on it was approximately forty thousand lower than mine, I knew he had been there quite some time.

I walked over and spoke to him. He told me he was a physician.

"Can you tell me what might have happened to my mother, my two little sisters and the rest of the people they took away last night?" I asked, searching his face for some glimmer of hope.

Without saying a word, he pointed away to the left.

In the distance, flames and smoke poured from massive trenches that I had not even noticed before. In that instant, I not only noticed them, I became transfixed by them. The flames seemed to pour from the bowels of the earth, the very pit of hell itself. And the smell from the billowing smoke was suddenly overwhelmingly nauseating. You can describe the smoke and flames, but you can never adequately describe that sickening smell.

With great sadness in his eyes he said, "That's what happened to them."

His words pierced my heart, shocking me to my core. I felt as if I had been struck on the head with a stone or injected with some kind of powerful drug. I was not myself. My brain churned in a chaotic storm of terror, rage, hatred, loss and guilt.

This cannot be real I thought, finally realizing the fate of my mother, sisters and the others whom the Nazis marched into the darkness just the night before.

In utter desperation, I silently asked, "Where is God?"

That was the only time I ever spoke God's name during the entire time I was a prisoner.

Without another word the older prisoner turned and walked away, leaving me alone with the truth I had been too naive to see or imagine. The old prisoner's words, "That's what happened to them," stripped my soul bare of any hope of seeing my family again.

Those words convinced me from that point on, that life for me was meaningless.

Slave Labor

It's amazing that we managed to live.

Working took tremendous effort, and our starvation diet was slowly killing us.

The Nazis were in a hurry to enlarge the capacity of the Auschwitz-Birkenau concentration camp because they had plans to fill it quickly with thousands of Jews and other prisoners as they implemented their "final solution" to the "Jewish problem."

They designed each barrack to hold five hundred to six hundred prisoners. The barracks, originally designed and prefabricated for use as horse stables, consisted of wooden walls, a roof and a dirt floor. The only windows were very small ones near the roof, which allowed a small amount of light to come in.

They were simple to assemble, which was our job most of the time. But some days they merely worked us to keep us occupied and exhausted. Sometimes they made us move dirt or stones, all by hand with no shovels, wheelbarrows or anything. Sometimes, the next day, they'd make us move it all back.

We were allowed no breaks and were given no water or food. From around eight in the morning until just before dark, they drove us to the point of collapse and beyond.

Every day we worked, even though we were starving, wet, cold, exhausted and often sick. The whole month of November was rainy. With no clothes to change into, we never got to wear anything dry. Of course we never got to bathe.

There was no room on our bunk to stretch or move and absolutely no privacy. If one prisoner coughed or moved, the other four felt it. We were so worn out that even though we were wet and hungry, it wasn't difficult to fall asleep.

The Nazis were not concerned about making life more comfortable for us. Our only purpose in life was to serve our Nazi masters as slave laborers to build barracks as fast as humanly possible. They used us until we dropped from exhaustion or until we simply refused to move further. When one of us could no longer work he was shot, whipped, beaten to death, or taken to the gas chambers. He was then immediately replaced with someone new.

At that time, there were thousands upon thousands of prisoners available for work. When the replacements were murdered, still more replacements were added to the force.

It was an existence completely devoid of hope. Simple instinct led us to try to make it through one more day, or one more hour, or even one more minute.

At some point I learned that my father was still alive in the camp. I occasionally saw him on work details. One day I saw him leaning against the wall of Barrack No. 7 and noticed that he appeared to be injured.

Barrack No. 7 was a holding area for prisoners who could no longer work and were scheduled to be executed in the gas chambers. I had already developed the fighting resistance within me. I went over to speak to him.

My father told me that he had fallen off a scaffold and broken his leg. We both knew that he would not be alive much longer.

"Samuel," he said to me, "I have lived most of my life, but you are still so young. Do everything you can do to stay alive."

It was a plea but not an emotional one, even though we both knew it was the end for him. I knew that I would follow my father ... the next day, next week, next month ... but surely would die. Knowing it removed all fear from my life.

And feeling.

Neither he nor I shed any tears. We no longer had tears to shed.

That was the last time I saw my father.

He was taken to the gas chamber that same day.

Survival Against All Odds

It may seem hard to understand, but after being exposed to so much brutality our emotions totally shut down. It was only after liberation that I was able to return to being a human being with normal human feelings and values.

As I think about my father today, I feel more emotion now than I felt on the day I said "goodbye" to him.

The agony was just too much to handle. You couldn't change the circumstances but you could change how you reacted to the circumstances.

For some, the only reaction left was to give in and give up. Many who reached their physical and emotional limits just committed suicide. They ran into the electrified fence that separated the compounds. They acted in ways forbidden by the Nazis so they would be shot.

This was an easily accomplished suicide. The SS guards appeared to take great pleasure in shooting those who could not keep up. Each day, they would whip, beat and kill prisoners who could not maintain the hectic pace of barracks construction.

SS guards, regardless of their rank, held absolute power of life or death over us. If they decided to shoot or beat a prisoner, their superiors never questioned it. The most important thing for the Nazis was that the number of dead prisoners when added to the number of live prisoners matched the overall number assigned to the camp. We were nothing more than inventory, and the only thing that mattered was the accuracy of their headcount.

Our days consisted of a never ending routine: being counted again and again, being forced to work and being systematically starved, beaten and humiliated. Physical beatings killed more prisoners than bullets. During the occupation, we had become accustomed to being screamed and shouted at, but in the camps if they wanted your attention they just hit you. It was total degradation in its vilest form.

Sometimes, after a brutally long day on work detail, some of the more sadistic SS guards would order us to line up outside the barrack and force us to do punishment exercises for hours until we literally collapsed from exhaustion. You could tell by their eyes that the punishment exercises served as a form of entertainment. When a prisoner finally collapsed, the SS guards subjected him to a terrible beating, or in many cases, simply shot him.

One night during the early months of my imprisonment, after a particularly brutal day of exhausting labor, I can remember lying on my pallet thinking that if only I could get a loaf of bread and eat it, I would be happy to fall asleep and never wake up.

Although I never actually contemplated suicide during the years I spent as a prisoner of the Nazis, I sometimes found myself thinking that it would not be a bad thing if I just passed away in my sleep.

I somehow managed, however, to exist one day at a time, never looking ahead and never looking back.

Death became a constant presence in our day-to-day existence. Each morning when we awoke, our first chore was to remove the bodies of our fellow prisoners who had died during the night. We carried their bodies outside, leaving them in rows next to the barrack. Then, we stood in our required formation. While some of the guards walked row to row, counting us as we stood, others added up the bodies of those who had died. It was most important to them that the numbers always be accurate.

Death also accompanied us on our daily slave labor work details. Each day, many prisoners were beaten or shot to death simply because they were no longer capable of working or had become sick or injured. Sometimes they were shot just because some SS guard took a personal dislike to them. Each time we lined up in our groups of five, the faces were different. So many people died from one day to the next that the order of our formations changed continually.

The Nazis' systematic program of death had taken first my brother and uncle, then my mother, sisters, aunts and several cousins. Death from slave labor had claimed my father and my brothers, Yussel and Srulek. On the increasingly rare occasions when I had the energy to think about it, I wondered when death would get around to claiming me, my brother Simon, my cousin Irving and my friends from Ciechanow.

Every day at Auschwitz, I saw trucks filled with innocent men, women and children from Jewish communities throughout Europe, all dressed in their best clothes, heading from "selection" at the train station directly to the gas chambers. I saw terrified families being torn apart. I saw brutal SS guards with dogs and whips herding thousands of elderly people and young mothers with infants and toddlers toward the gas chambers. I saw the Nazis marching physically fit men and women into different compounds assigned to slave labor details.

By then I knew that Auschwitz-Birkenau was designed to kill human beings. However, I didn't realize at that time just how efficient the Nazis had become. Recently, while reading "Auschwitz Chronicle 1939-1945," by Danuta Czech, I discovered an entry on page 265 that described the arrival of my family and our friends and neighbors from Ciechanow at Auschwitz-Birkenau on November 7, 1942:

"2,000 Jewish men, women and children arrive with an RSHA transport from the Zichenau ghetto in the so-called Administrative District of Zichenau (Ciechanow). After the selection, 465 men and 229 women are admitted to the camp and receive Nos. 73531-73995 and 23734-23962. The remaining 1,306 people are killed in the gas chambers."

My mother, sisters, aunts and cousins were among those 1,306 people the Nazis murdered during the night of November 7, 1942 before they could become "officially registered inmates" at the Auschwitz-Birkenau death camp. As I continued to read "Auschwitz Chronical 1939-1945," I discovered that of the 10,500 Jews transported from Ciechanow to Auschwitz during November 1942, the Nazis immediately killed 7,052 people without even officially counting them as inmates. While reading "Auschwitz 1270 to Present," by Deborah Dwork and Robert Jan van Pelt, I discovered the following information on page 253, which describes the horrible efficiency of the Nazi killing machine:

"In the twenty-three days between 12 November 1942 and 5 December, 1942, 2,000 prisoners were gassed, 461 sick inmates were killed with phenol injections, 25 were executed, 2 were shot 'in flight,' 1 was hanged and 1 was tortured to death. Another 837 people died as a result of 'natural causes' — starvation, exhaustion or a combination of both. This totaled 3,327 murdered human beings. The true situation was even more ghastly; these official statistics applied only to officially registered inmates. During the same twenty three days 13,000 people were sent immediately to the gas chambers of Bunkers 1 and 2 in Birkenau."

Birkenau Main Camp

A few weeks before Christmas 1942, I was constructing barracks when a friendly older Russian prisoner asked if I would work with him at night doing carpentry at the camp's main food warehouse.

"I'd like to come and get you tomorrow night," he said. "You'll like what you see."

Food.

I would have access to extra food if I helped him out, he promised. I had been on starvation rations for about a month, and I was so excited about the prospect of food that I could hardly sleep that night.

After roll call the next evening, the Russian came into the barracks.

"I'm taking 73538 with me to work at the food warehouse," he told the "barrack oldest." Since he did not object, we left.

I couldn't believe my eyes. I saw kettles filled with boiled potatoes, kettles filled with soup, hundreds of loaves of bread and hundreds of sacks of potatoes, just sitting there. Of course, I managed to help myself to some. I felt lucky to have that job, even if it was only going to be for a day or two.

I helped the Russian in the warehouse for a few evenings and continued to work my regular slave labor day job constructing barracks. It wasn't long until some other warehouse workers asked if I would help them in the evenings after my construction work was finished. They said I could clean and sweep the warehouse and run errands for them.

Knowing I would be able to get more food, I eagerly agreed. Every evening after returning from my work building barracks, I worked for several hours in the warehouse building shelves and doing other carpentry work. This extra job was very difficult to do after working all day on the barrack construction project, but it actually saved my life because it kept me from starving.

It also gave me an opportunity to provide extra food to my brother and my friends by leaving a bucket of potatoes, or some bread for them in a hiding place outside the warehouse from time to time. I was risking my life by stealing food for them, and they were risking their lives by taking it. To protect me, no matter how hungry they were, they never went near the place where I hid food if they thought anyone might see me.

At first I just worked the extra duty in the warehouse two or three nights a week. Eventually, they wanted me there every day. The guards didn't care where you worked as long as you worked.

Christmas Day, 1942

Christmas Day, 1942, was bitterly cold. The sun was shining brightly, but ice and snow covered the camp and the temperature was in the teens.

We did not have to go out to work that day, and there was a rumor that the guards would give us an extra piece of bread in our daily ration. This rumor raised our hopes that maybe the SS guards would be celebrating Christmas and would allow us to have a full day of rest.

The commander of our camp was not present that day. He left in charge his second in command, a sadist of the worst kind who always walked around with a vicious German Shepherd dog on the end of a leash. He took pleasure in ordering the dog to attack prisoners.

We soon found out that instead of giving us a day of rest, he and his sadistic guards had found yet another brutal way to torture us.

After we assembled outside the barrack for roll call that morning, the SS guards rounded up 200 or 300 of us and marched us out of the camp towards a huge pile of sand. At the pile the SS guards divided us into two groups. Those of us in one group were ordered to hold up the ends of our coats to make buckets while the others were ordered to drop shovels-full of sand onto our coats.

Then the SS forced us to run back into the camp and spread the sand on patches of ice and snow.

Very quickly, the SS turned this chore into a blood sport.

The SS guards and some prisoner kapos, most of whom were carrying shovel handles and pick handles, lined both sides of the main road through our camp.

Screaming, "faster, faster," they beat us while we ran through the gauntlet. When they hit a prisoner on the head and knocked him down, an SS guard placed the shovel handle across his neck, stepped on it, and strangled him to death.

They forced other prisoners to pick up the bodies and place them under the camp Christmas tree.

This was the one of the most macabre scenes I ever witnessed during my entire time in the concentration camps.

I guess the SS killed between fifteen and twenty prisoners carrying sand that day.

While I was lucky enough to avoid blows to my head, I took plenty of them across my shoulders, back and arms. After I had run that gauntlet for several hours, a senior prisoner who knew me pulled me out of the line and took me to another area to work. It was probably because of that prisoner's kindness that I survived the day.

About fifteen years ago, the German Embassy requested that I come to Washington, D.C., to identify the SS guards who had participated in this brutality.

Evidently, the embassy was investigating that atrocity and had potentially identified some of the SS personnel. I went to the embassy and looked at the pictures. I can still visualize nearly every detail of that horrible day, but the faces of individuals are lost to me. I looked at the names of the SS personnel but I was unable to make a positive identification.

Main Camp Warehouse

A few weeks after Christmas 1942, the Nazis moved me into a barrack that contained hundreds of Russian prisoners of war. Those prisoners did not wear the standard prisoner stripes; rather they continued to wear their Russian uniforms from which all rank insignia had been removed. The Russians did that so the Nazis would never know who the senior officers and non-commissioned officers were.

These Russian POWs were an extremely tough group of men assigned by the Nazis to a work detail stripping salvageable materials off crashed planes stored near Birkenau. While doing their jobs, some drank the plane fuel and marched back to camp in a drunken stupor.

I became friendly with many of those Russian prisoners and they taught me to speak Russian fluently. Whenever the Nazis assigned new groups of Russian prisoners to the camp, I was able to converse with them in several different dialects.

The reason I was moved to the Russian barrack was because I now had a regular job at the main camp warehouse, where I had been working at night. One of my duties was to run from barrack to barrack announcing that the daily soup was ready for pickup.

I worked hard all day long, making sure that my areas of responsibility were always clean and ready for inspection. At that time, I was the only Jewish prisoner working in the main camp warehouse.

Early in 1943, the SS supervisor in charge of the camp warehouses came in to inspect. He was a large, mean redhead who always had a cigar stuck in his mouth. He was the type of SS man that everyone tried to avoid.

When he saw the Star of David on my chest, he shouted in German, "Throw the Jew out!"

The head man in the warehouse, a non-Jewish prisoner, called me over and said: "Samuel, I don't have any choice, you really should leave, but I'll take a chance on you. Just make sure you hide behind a column whenever that bastard comes in again."

I continued work there, making sure I stayed away from the office. Several times I saw that SS officer come into the warehouse. I tried very hard to keep out of his sight, but in spite of my efforts, he did see me a few times.

For some reason he didn't say anything to me or to the warehouse supervisor who had given me a second chance.

One day, a truck arrived at the warehouse loaded with heavy sacks of flour. That SS officer spotted me and called me into his office. I ran to him, removed my hat and stood at rigid attention. Pretending to show respect was just part of the routine for survival.

He ordered me to help another prisoner who was unloading the truck. Each sack of flour weighed 100 kilograms or 221 pounds. At that time I weighed 110 pounds. When I put the first sack on flour on my shoulders, my knees began to buckle. But I was determined to carry that sack into the warehouse. When finally I succeeded, I dropped the flour sack to the floor, straightened my shaking spine and went back for a second sack. On the way back into the warehouse, my knees buckled more with each step. I knew I would not be able to carry many more sacks without collapsing on the floor.

And I knew that if I fell, the redheaded SS man would shoot me.

As I headed back to the truck for my third sack, he shouted at me to come back into the office. Again, I stood before him at rigid attention with my hat in my hand.

"How old are you?" he asked.

"Twenty seven years old, sir," I answered. Of course, I was only eighteen, but I wasn't about to tell him that. I wanted him to think that I was mature enough for warehouse work.

"From now on, you are going to work at the quarantine camp warehouse," he said.

I think I must have impressed him with my determination. I'm sure he didn't like assigning the job to a Jew, but it must have been more important to him to get the warehouse work done properly.

Malinka

Throughout a lifetime, a few special people remain in our memories forever.

Late in 1942, I met a man whose nickname was "Malinka," from the city of Krakow.

When I asked him why he was in Birkenau, he said that he had been in jail in Krakow for stealing a cow, and the Germans brought him here.

Malinka was a tough guy who wasn't afraid of anyone or anything. While in Birkenau, he worked with my brother, Simon, and some other friends repairing barracks roofs.

While the others actually worked, Malinka looked for ways to wheel and deal.

He and my brother spent many days "repairing" the roof of the bread warehouse while I was working there. While one kept watch, the other lowered an empty bucket through a skylight. I filled the bucket with bread and sent it back up to them.

Throughout the camp, there was a certain amount of black market activity going on.

Prisoners assigned to the crematorium detail had found money on the bodies removed from the gas chambers, and it circulated among the prisoners.

A guard who worked in the kitchen occasionally smuggled sausage to Malinka, and he, in turn, sold it to prisoners.

One day, that guard approached me.

"Samuel," he said, "tell Malinka that he owes me money for the sausage."

When I told Malinka, he just shrugged. "Tell him not to worry about it."

That was so typical of Malinka's attitude. He simply didn't worry about anything, even though he knew that the guard held the power of life or death over him.

Not long afterward, a prisoner in the adjoining camp asked Malinka if he had any sausage to sell. Malinka showed him a sausage and arranged a sale. While the prisoner was getting his money, Malinka found a three-legged milking stool, broke off one of the legs and wrapped it so it looked like a sausage.

At the appointed time, Malinka took the wrapped piece of wood to the prisoner, who was standing on the other side of a fence.

As soon as he had collected his money, Malinka said "Watch out, the guards are coming," and walked away. He now had enough money to pay the guard.

On another occasion, Malinka stole my brother's boots one night and sold them to another prisoner. When my brother woke up the next morning, his boots were gone. Later, Malinka finally admitted to my brother what he had done.

In late 1944, Malinka was transfered to the Theresianstadt concentration camp in Czechoslovakia. After liberation, I caught up with him in Munich and we remained close friends until his death in New York in the 1980s.

Quarantine Camp Warehouse

The quarantine camp was the place where new prisoners were held for two to three weeks until they could be reassigned to the main camp or shipped out. By this time, however, there was no more room in the main camp — it was full. Birkenou proper now held from 50,000 to 70,000 prisoners, 15,000 of whom were women.

The quarantine camp was the smallest of all the camps. It had only one row of barracks where 2,000 to 3,000 prisoners were housed.

As the prisoner in charge of the quarantine camp bread storage warehouse, I was responsible for ensuring that the bread and potato inventory was accurate.

The warehouse had a concrete floor, and the food was stacked on wooden pallets. A blackboard hung on one wall and I kept the inventory by writing the counts on it with chalk.

Of course, the inventory was never accurate. Fairly regularly, I managed to sneak extra portions of food to my brother, Simon, my cousin, Irving, and a few friends I could trust.

On the chalkboard, I wrote down what the inventory was supposed to be, not what it actually was. At one time, I know it was at least 150 loaves short.

At first, nothing was locked, and while I had to be careful, I slept on a straw sack in a room near the entrance and could get food out pretty easily. Then they put everything under lock and key, and the task became harder and harder.

They never counted the bread themselves, and I stacked the pallets in such a way that they never knew.

But inside the perfect mountains of bread, there were numerous holes. If the SS guards ever discovered the shortages during a surprise inventory, the Nazis would have shot me instantly. I was positive I would never survive.

The Nazis allocated one quarter of a loaf of bread daily to each prisoner. The term "loaf" is very misleading. These loaves were not the size we buy in today's supermarket. They were approximately the size of the small loaves placed on the tables in restaurants. One can simply imagine how impossible it was for prisoners to survive on the daily ration of one quarter of a very small loaf.

One day, the senior SS warehouse supervisor ordered me to prepare the bread to be delivered to each barrack. He told me that Barrack No. 8 was to receive 135 loaves and I called back to him the same number to confirm it.

This meant that there were 540 prisoners assigned to that barrack and that each of them was to receive one quarter of a loaf.

I started loading the bread containers two loaves at a time. Wanting to sneak some extra bread to the barrack, I looked up to see what the SS supervisor was doing. I noticed that while he was not looking directly at me, he was listening intently. Instead of watching me, he was keeping track of the count by listening to the sound of the bread going into the containers.

The opportunity thrilled me. I liked nothing better than outsmarting the Nazis every chance I got, so I decided to take the challenge. Eight times, instead of grabbing two loaves, I grabbed three at a time. This meant that Barrack No. 8 was going to get some much-needed extra bread that day.

Of the eight extra loaves, four had to be given as a bribe to the "barrack oldest," and my brother and his friends could divide the remaining four. Of course, the risk was that the SS supervisor could have ordered me to empty the container and count the loaves in front of him. Lucky for me, this never happened, and I continued to steal extra food whenever it was possible.

Stealing provided us with the means to survive the starvation and torture imposed by the Nazis. The theft of a small piece of bread, or an extra piece of potato, or an extra spoonful of soup gave us the incentive and strength to get through that particular day and night.

Many of us became expert at stealing everything that wasn't under the direct observation of the Nazis.

It was a challenge to do anything you could do to "break the law." Our survival depended on our willingness to take the risks associated with thievery.

We had to be clever, and we had to be willing to act in an instant. The attraction of stealing was not only a matter of getting the necessary food; it was also a way we could feel the self-respect that came from outwitting our oppressors. We became addicted to stealing, and, in fact, after liberation many of us found it difficult to curtail the desire to steal, even though it was no longer a necessity.

Each camp had a number of highly skilled craftsmen in confinement. There were shoemakers, tailors, cabinetmakers and so forth.

The Nazis used these craftsmen to make special uniforms, boots and furniture. I became friendly with a talented shoemaker and occasionally gave him an extra piece of bread or potato. In return, he created a wonderful pair of leather boots for me out of pieces of good leather that the Nazis collected in the camp. It was wonderful to get rid of those dried-up old shoes that cut my feet so badly they bled.

The main bakery was in Auschwitz, and every day, a truck would come loaded with our ration of bread. One day, the SS guard who made the delivery noticed my new boots.

While we unloaded and counted that day's bread, he called me over. I stood at attention before him, cap in hand.

He pointed at my feet and asked if I could have a pair made for him. I told him I could and sent for the shoemaker. When the shoemaker arrived, he took the SS guard's foot measurements and left without a word spoken between them. A few days later, the shoemaker delivered a brand new pair of leather boots to me. I hid them until the SS guard arrived with the bread. When I presented the boots to him, he said nothing but it was obvious that he was very pleased.

The incident of the boots must have convinced the guard that I could get things done in the camp. Shortly afterward, he asked if I could have a uniform made for him. I sent for the tailor who silently took his measurements and left. The guard brought in some old uniforms, which the tailor then remade into a very fine uniform.

When the guard made his next bread delivery there was a brand new tailored uniform waiting for him. Again, he did not express any appreciation but it was obvious that he was pleased. That guard thought he was the best-dressed man in the camp.

A few days later, the SS guard made another bread delivery. As usual he dropped the bread off and left without saying anything to me. To my surprise, when I counted the loaves to add them to the inventory I discovered fifty extra.

This was like a miracle. It came just in time to help me replenish the inventory shortage I had created by giving extra rations to my brother, cousin and friends. Every so often, that guard would continue to add fifty extra loaves to his delivery. I believe that those extra rations of bread enabled some of us to survive the Nazis' systematic program of starvation.

I wouldn't say the guard was nice, but he at least had some honor. The vicious redhead SS guard in charge of the warehouses, however, went out of his way to make life more miserable for the prisoners. One day he came into the warehouse and found dust on the rafters. I had told the other prisoners who worked in the warehouse to make sure everything was always ready for inspection. In addition, I told them that if they ever punished me because the guard found dust or any other discrepancies, I did not want to see any of them there when I got back.

On that particular day, the red-headed guard told me to report to him at the main camp kitchen. When I got there, he made me do punishment exercises for an hour. While I was doing the exercises the SS guard who was in charge of the main camp kitchen tried to help me out. He could not do much because the redhead was watching. The kitchen guard was a decent guy, not a brutal bastard like the redhead.

When I finished the exercises I walked back to the quarantine camp warehouse and told the other prisoners what had happened. After that experience, I made sure the other prisoners assigned to my warehouse kept the place ready for inspection at all times.

One of the prisoners who worked in the warehouse with me was a Polish political prisoner named Stashek who came from the city of Katowitz. Although he was several years older, we became good friends.

One day, we found out that Stashek was scheduled for transport out of Birkenau. In our experience, any change from the routine turned out to be a change for the worse. It was unlikely that this transport was good news. So I went to another prisoner friend, who worked in the camp office, and asked him if there was any way he could remove Stashek's name from the transport list. My office friend must have found a way because Stashek remained in Birkenau.

A year or so after my liberation from Dachau, I wrote a letter to Stashek's father in Katowitz to find out if he had gotten out of the camps alive. His father wrote back that the Americans had liberated Stashek. He thanked me for helping save his son's life.

However, after telling me how grateful he was, he went on to say that my kindness "was such a rare thing for a Jew to do."

I wrote back and asked him how many Jewish people he ever had contact with that made him feel like that. He never replied. His comment was indicative of the ingrained prejudice against Jews that was prevalent throughout Eastern Europe at that time and is still prevalent among many people today.

Christmas, 1943

By Christmas 1943, I was in charge of the warehouse where they distributed the bread and the kitchen where they made the soup.

Guards were there all the time, twelve hours a day.

The day before Christmas, three or four prisoners were working with me in the kitchen, the SS Guards were there and also the SS Sergeant in charge of the camp.

Since it was the holiday season, and the SS Guards were feeling in a festive mood, they smuggled a few bottles of whiskey into the quarantine camp kitchen. The prisoner in charge of the kitchen passed the bottle around to all the prisoners, and by the end of the afternoon, we were all feeling quite drunk. You can just imagine what raw whiskey does to an empty stomach. Besides, I had never drunk whiskey in my life.

One of the guards came in, saw what was going on, and decided to join in the fun. He called me over to him and offered me a drink. I stood at attention with my hat in my hand and told him that I didn't drink. He could tell just by looking at me that I had been drinking earlier but I learned early in camp life that you never admitted to anything. Never. I continued to refuse to drink with him and he eventually went away without punishing me.

After he left, the Polish prisoner in charge made us sing Christmas carols for hours. We knew nothing about these songs, but we repeated those carols over and over so many times that I remembered all the verses.

It must have been quite a sight to see that emaciated group of drunken Jewish and Polish prisoners singing carols at the top of their lungs.

The good thing about that incident was that the whiskey helped us to momentarily forget our problems, and no one was punished for it.

A Visit to the Women's Camp

Several rows of electrified fences separated my camp from the women's camp at Birkenau. There were guards in watchtowers, and guards patrolled the perimeters with dogs. The security inside and outside the compounds was extremely tight in order to prevent escapes.

One day, while my friend and I were talking, he suggested that we try to get into the Women's Camp to see some of our friends from home.

Shortly after we had arrived at Auschwitz, my construction barrack was ordered to do some work in the women's camp. My first sight of the women's camp during those early months was one of the few things that penetrated my shock and numbness. By then we men were accustomed to the inhumanity around us. You dragged the dead out of your barrack in the morning. You preoccupied yourself with getting food, or something with which to make a pair of socks.

But even so, we were not prepared to see that the women were living under the same conditions. Their heads were shaved, they wore prison uniforms, they slogged through the mud, froze, starved and did all the work that the men did. You grew up to respect and care for women. The effect of seeing them in that condition was devastating to most of us.

Later, when my friend proposed the visit, we had become accustomed even to the women's degradation. We were simply doing our best to figure out a way to survive.

I told my friend that I would think about the visit and try to come up with a plan. I also told him not to say one word to anyone else that we were thinking about it. The situation in the camp was no different from the occupation. You simply could not take a chance of having the wrong person find out that you had planned to "break the law." I fully understood that we would be taking a very serious risk in just attempting to get into that camp.

After thinking about it for awhile, I told my friend that we would try it that night. A few weeks earlier I had found a voltage tester that I used to find out which wires were hot. After dark, we crept to the fence and used a two-by-four piece of wood to hook onto the lowest strand of barbed wire and keep it separated from the electrically charged wire. While holding the wire up with the wood, we then scooped out some dirt until we made a depression large enough to allow us to crawl under the wires. Being as thin as we were, we did not need a very large hole to get under the fence.

We repeated the process several times because there was more than one fence separating the two compounds.

After crawling under the last wire, we spent a few minutes visiting with our friends and telling stories of what we had been going through. Then it was time to backtrack under the fences and try to remove all traces that someone had been there.

The next day we saw the guards inspecting the fence line all around the women's camp. We learned they were searching for a woman who was missing from roll call.

Of course, they found the fresh dirt in the places we had crawled through and they assumed that the missing woman was being hidden in the men's camp. The SS immediately ordered all the prisoners in camp to line up outside the barracks while they conducted a full-scale search of both the women's camp and ours. We stood for a couple of hours while the guards frantically searched for the missing woman. During that time, other SS guards walked among us demanding that we come forward and tell them where we were hiding the woman. Of course, no one moved forward and neither my friend nor I dared to look at each other. We knew that the SS were getting angrier by the minute.

Eventually, they found the missing woman sleeping in another part of the women's camp and they called off the search. My friend and I were extremely lucky that the Nazis did not catch us that night. After that incident, we made no further visits to the women's camp.

An Informant

In late November 1944, the Nazis transported a group of Czech Jews to Auschwitz.

By that time, we noticed that the transports were not arriving as frequently as they had been in the past. Of course, we did not know the reason for the slowdown. We speculated it might be because there were not that many Jews remaining in Europe. Of course, we did not have access to news of the war. We just sensed that things might not be going well for the Nazis.

Unlike previous transports, this group, which consisted of families with small infants and children, as well as elderly men and women, was not immediately "selected" for either work or death. Rather, they were all kept together in the compound next to my compound.

I was very impressed by this group; they reminded me of my family and friends during the occupation. I stole small quantities of milk and bread and smuggled it across the fence to try to help them provide food for their babies. After I did this for a few days and they began to trust me, I learned that they were from Prague. When I asked them how they had avoided capture for so long, they told me that people hid them in different locations throughout Prague. However, a Jewish informant had told the Nazis where their hiding places were. They told me they did not know why, but they speculated that his motivation was self-preservation. When I asked what happened to the informant, they said the Nazis transported him with their group and he was in the camp with them now.

I asked for his name and they told me. It was another case of the Nazi's making use of an informant to get information they wanted and then turning around and double-crossing the informant.

After a few days, the Nazis put that group of Czech Jews through the "selection" process. The Nazis sent men and women capable of working to separate men and women's camps, while the elderly, the sick, the infants and children were marched directly into the gas chambers. When I found out that the Nazis sent the informant to the men's camp, I was able to get word to that camp about what he had done to his fellow Jews. Of course, I did not witness anything, but I am sure he did not survive the night. An informant simply did not survive in the concentration camps.

If that despicable person had not informed on them, they might have survived the rest of war hiding in Prague.

In all my years in the camps, I had never broken down and cried, even when I found out the fate of my family. However, on the day those Czech Jews were "selected," I watched the Nazis march those beautiful people off to the gas chambers, and I wept.

An Unusual SS Officer

Late one night, during the latter part of 1944, one of the SS camp officers came to the room near the warehouse entrance where I slept. As usual, there was no knock, he just walked in. As I heard his footsteps I jumped up and stood at attention.

"Relax," he said to me in German. "Is there anyone else here? I need to talk to you."

I let him know we were alone, and he continued.

"I want to know if there is any way that I can alleviate the pressure on some of the prisoners here? Find out what you can and let me know. Just remember, when you see me during the day, you are a prisoner and I am the commander. I'll be back."

His visit and his offer to help us absolutely shocked me. I had no idea what he was up to or what his motives were, and I really did not know what to do. At first, I thought he might be trying to set us up somehow. I later decided to find out if his offer to help was genuine.

I became aware of one barrack that was crowded with more than 500 prisoners, many of whom were abused mercilessly by the prisoner in charge, the "barrack oldest." This person was a German political prisoner sentenced to the camp. He wasn't a Jew. I do not know why he was confined, but that did not matter because he was still a prisoner.

Several prisoners from that barrack came to me and told me what was going on. Their "barrack oldest" reduced their bread rations by cutting them in half. I do not know what he did with the extra bread. He could have sold it or traded it for some kind of personal gain.

He also beat the prisoners for no reason at all and forced them to perform punishment exercises. When I found out what he was doing, I confronted him and asked why he was mistreating the others.

"Samuel, you're my friend," he looked at me and said. "Why do you care what I do?"

Disgusted, I just walked away. I then decided to report the man to the SS officer if he ever again visited me in the warehouse.

Several nights after his first visit, the SS officer came back to the warehouse. Once again he asked me if there was anything he could do to help us. I told him about the situation in that other barrack, and he asked me to see if the other prisoners would give me their smaller portions of bread for use as evidence.

So I went to the other prisoners and asked them to give me their bread the next time the "barrack oldest" shorted them. I did not tell them what I was going to do with the bread, and they did not ask.

Later, they gave me some pieces of the reduced bread rations and I gave them to the SS officer.

I still didn't know if he was serious about helping.

A few days later, we found out that the senior SS commander of the entire camp had arrested that "barrack oldest" and transferred him into the "punishment kommando." This was a group of prisoners isolated into a separate barrack, where the prisoners were required to perform the most severe hard labor in the concentration camp system.

This was the only time I knew any SS officer to in anyway help or try to make life easier for the prisoners. To this day, I still do not know what motivated him. Perhaps it was because he sensed that the war was coming to an end, or perhaps he had a guilty conscience.

After the war, the French military captured that SS officer. He told the French authorities there was a prisoner named Samuel who had worked in the Birkenau warehouse who knew what he had done to help some prisoners there. He told the French military to try to contact me.

The French military tribunal found out through some of my contemporaries that I was living in Munich and sent a subpoena for me to come to the French sector of occupied Germany to testify. On the appointed day, they brought that SS officer, bound in chains, before the French military tribunal. They called me forward, and I told them the story of how the "barrack oldest" cheated the prisoners out of their bread ration. I also said the SS officer had volunteered to help us by having that "barrack oldest" transferred to the punishment kommando.

As they led the SS officer from the courtroom, he turned his head towards me and said "Thank you, Samuel."

That was the last time I saw or heard anything about him, and I have no idea of the results of his trial. Some of my contemporaries were critical of my testimony and told me that I should not have said anything in his favor. However, the fact of the matter was that he was the only SS officer who ever tried to help us, and I felt obligated to tell the truth about him.

Resistance Movement

It is a misperception that most of the Jewish prisoners of the Nazis went meekly to their deaths without offering any resistance. When one considers that our Nazi keepers had absolute control over every single aspect of our existence, one understands that there were very few opportunities for any form of successful resistance. However, many of the Jewish prisoners, acting individually or in groups, did everything humanly possible to create problems for the Nazis, knowing full well that getting caught meant instant torture and death.

In Auschwitz-Birkenau, there was an organized resistance movement that operated in a highly secret manner. My connection to that movement was through a prisoner who worked as a clerk in the warehouse office. He kept track of the prisoners assigned to the Quarantine Camp.

One day, that prisoner asked me to walk outside with him. He told me that the Russians had plans to drop paratroopers into the camp. When that happened, I was to open the doors to the barracks, lead the prisoners to try to cut through the fence and attempt to disarm the guards in the guardhouse.

Of course, we realized that many of us would probably be shot down, but we felt that at least some of us would survive a mass escape attempt.

The general feeling was that we really didn't have anything to lose but our lives, and most of us believed that sooner or later we would die from starvation anyhow. Three weeks later, he told me that they scrapped the plan because there were too many sick prisoners that would have to be left behind. I have no idea where he got his information or how many other prisoners had knowledge of it. It was the only time I was approached by anyone to participate in such a plan.

A more active resistance movement was led by prisoners assigned to the Sonderkommando. These were the special squads whose job was to operate the crematoriums.

I remember the first occasion when I saw the sonderkommando chosen. I had just arrived at the camp, and we were all lined up for work assignment. We were told that this particular group sorted clothing and were given extra food. I hoped to be chosen and was sorry they said I was too small for the job.

We had no idea what the Sonderkommando did.

Later, one of the Sonderkommando brought me extra food. It turned out that they worked for six months, then were executed and replaced.

My first cousin, Shimon Altus, also from Ciechanow, was assigned to that unit and participated in the active resistance there.

The following is quoted from an entry dated October 7, 1944, on pages 725-726 in "Auschwitz Chronicle 1939-1945," by Danuta Czech:

"On Saturday morning, the camp resistance movement informs the leader of the Auschwitz Combat Group, who is in the Special Squad, that news has been obtained about the camp management's plans to liquidate as quickly as possible the surviving members of the Special Squad.

"This news probably confirms the information that the operation, announced a few days ago by the SS, to reduce the size of the Special Squads of Crematoriums IV and V by 300 named prisoners allegedly slated for a transport, is to be carried out.

"The named prisoners decide to mount a resistance. At the midday break, during a conference in Crematorium IV, the staff of the Special Squad Combat Group is surprised by a German BV prisoner, who threatens to report them to the SS.

"The informer is killed on the spot.

"At 1:25 p.m., the threatened group attacks the approaching SS guard unit with hammers, axes, and stones. They set Crematorium IV on fire and throw several self-made grenades.

"Afterward, some of the prisoners from Squad 59B reach the small wooded area nearby. At the same time, the prisoners of Squad 57B, who work in Crematorium II, become active.

"When they see the flames and hear the shooting, they believe this is the signal for the general uprising of the prisoners in the camp. They overpowered the Head Kapo, a Reich German, and push him and an SS man whom they have disarmed, into the burning crematorium oven. They beat to death a second SS man, tear up the fence that surrounds the crematorium area, and flee.

"The prisoners of Squads 58B and 60B in Crematoriums III and IV undertake nothing because some of them are not informed about the plans, and also because the SS men there bring the situation quickly under control. The immediate intervention by the SS guards, the surrounding of the crematorium compound, and the heavy machine-gun and artillery fire in the direction of the small woods near Crematorium IV, where the prisoners mount a resistance, quickly squelches the uprising.

"In Rajsko, pursuing SS men block the way of the fleeing prisoners of Squad 57B. The prisoners barricade themselves in a barn and prepare to resist. The SS men set the barn on fire and murder the prisoners. Two hundred and fifty prisoners die in this battle, among them the organizers of the uprising.

"A fire-fighting squad is sent from Auschwitz I to put out the fire in Crematorium IV. These prisoners, who put out the fire under the supervision of the SS, are witnesses to the suppression of the uprising by the SS and the shooting to death of the members of Squad 59B.

"The fire-fighting squad is then brought to Rajsko, to put out the fire in the barn. An air-raid alarm prevents the SS men from further pursuit.

"In the evening, all the prisoners who were killed are brought to the grounds of Crematorium IV and the remaining members of the Special Squad are driven together. Another 200 prisoners from the squads that took part in the uprising are shot to death.

"A representative of the Commandant delivers a threatening speech in which he announces that if there is a repetition of such incidents, all prisoners in the camp will be shot to death. Afterward, work is resumed in Crematoriums II, III and V. During the uprising three SS men are killed by the prisoners."

Immediately after the uprising, the SS launched a massive investigation to determine how the prisoners were able to get their hands on sufficient quantities of explosives to make the hand grenades.

Their investigation focused on the female prisoners who worked at a factory that made ammunition for the Nazi war effort. I quote the following information from an entry dated October 10, 1944, on pages 738-729 of "Auschwitz Chronicle 1939-1945," by Danuta Czech:

"Three female Jewish prisoners employed in the Weichsel-Union-Metallwerke, Ella Gartner, Ester Wajsblum and Ragina Safin, are arrested in the women's camp of Auschwitz I. They are charged with stealing explosives from the depot of the plant and of giving them to the prisoners of the Special Squad. With the explosive, the prisoners fashioned primitive grenades that they used during the uprising of October 7.

"Two more female prisoners are arrested in the women's camp of Auschwitz II (Birkenau) on the charge of having contact with the Special Squad and transporting explosives there. One of those arrested, the female Polish Jew Roza Robota, works in the personal effects camp, which borders on the compound of Crematorium IV. Roza Robota accepted from one of her fellow prisoners, explosive material stolen by Ella Gartner in the Weichsel-Union plant and passed it on to (prisoner) Wrobel of the Special Squad."

Roza Robota, who was a few years older than me, grew up in Ciechanow, and was a very close friend. The marriage of my uncle David Altus to Roza's aunt connected our families.

According to additional information on page 729 of "Auschwitz Chronicle 1939-1945," Roza refused to provide information concerning prisoner Wrobel until she was certain that the Nazis had already killed him. After withstanding three months of brutal interrogations, the Nazis hanged her. The following is quoted from page 775, "Auschwitz Chronicle 1939-1945":

"In the evening, four female Jewish prisoners, Ella Gartner, Roza Robota, Regina Safir, and Estera Wajsblum, are hanged in the women's camp of Auschwitz. They were condemned to death because they assisted in the uprising that broke out on October 7, 1944, among the members of the Special Squad in the crematoriums in Birkenau. They provided the Special Squad with explosives and munitions from the depots of the Weichsel-Union-Metallwerke, where three of the women worked.

"The execution takes place in two stages. Two female prisoners are hanged during the evening roll call in the presence of the male and female prisoners who work the night shift at Weichsel-Union. The other two female prisoners are hanged after the return of the squad that works the day shift. The reason for the sentence is read by First Protective Custody Commander Hossler in Auschwitz; he screams that all traitors will be destroyed in this manner."

Although the above actions constituted a major form of resistance, there were countless lesser acts of heroism by thousands of prisoners working alone or in small groups to disrupt the Nazis' command and control functions in the camps.

One of those heroic acts involved an American Jewish woman who had been "selected" to go to the gas chambers. When she and the other women were ordered to undress, she removed her blouse, but refused to remove her bra. An SS guard pulled his pistol out and attempted to remove her bra. She knocked the pistol out of his hand, picked it up and shot him to death. Of course, she was immediately killed and sent to the crematorium.

Other acts of resistance, such as slowing down barrack construction, sabotaging facilities, and so forth, were carried out anonymously on a regular basis by prisoners who were willing to risk their lives just to make life more difficult for the Nazis. Those prisoners, acting alone or in small groups, were very clever and secretive in guarding their resistance plans from the extensive informant network the Nazis had in place throughout the camps.

PART FOUR

Dachau

The Journey to Dachau

In January 1945, while the Russians were approaching from the East, the Nazis had been marching many prisoners out of the large camps at Auschwitz-Birkenau.

In early January, the Nazis closed a section of my camp at Birkenau and transferred me to the main Auschwitz-Birkenau camp where I went back to work in the main warehouse.

One day I had an opportunity to steal a case of margarine. At that time, hijacking a case of margarine was equal to hijacking Fort Knox, but I did it and got away with it.

After I divided it among my friends, a German criminal prisoner came up to me.

"I saw what you did, Samuel," he said. "What about me?"

I told him that he did not see anything, and he was not going to get anything. One thing you learned quickly was that you never backed down if threatened by another prisoner.

He looked hard at me, pointed his finger and said, "I'm going to get you, remember that."

I knew what he meant. He intended to kill me.

I was a little guy, weighing only 110 pounds. I had a lot of mouth, but I knew that physically I would not be a match for that guy.

One evening a few days later, as I was handing out bread to a group of prisoners who were being marched out of Birkenau, I thought about his threat and realized that he was serious about killing me.

I made a quick decision to leave. As it got darker, I grabbed a loaf of bread, shoved it under my arm, pushed a guy aside and jumped into the line of prisoners who were marching out the gate.

I had no idea where we were going, but I knew if I stayed in Birkenau, the German prisoner would probably find an opportunity to kill me.

Just over a stick of margarine.

After marching away from Birkenau, our group met up with a group of prisoners moving out of the main camp at Auschwitz. There were now several hundred prisoners being marched away from the Auschwitz-Birkenau complex by the Nazis. We trudged through snow all night without stopping. We were freezing cold and thoroughly miserable. Adding to our misery was the fact we had no idea where we were going.

Not that it mattered to me. All I cared about was getting away from the German prisoner who intended to kill me.

That march was so severe that the SS guards shot some prisoners and even shot a few of their own guards who could not keep up the pace.

After we marched for awhile, one of the SS guards told me to carry a rucksack for him. When I threw the rucksack over my shoulders, I heard the sound of bottles clinking. As the night went on and we continued to march without taking a break, I became very, very thirsty. I thought there might be something to drink in the bottles in that rucksack, so I grabbed one of the bottles, opened it and shared it with the prisoner walking next to me. It tasted great.

Later we shared the other bottle. When I was sure that no one was watching, I tossed the rucksack and the empty bottles into the forest to get rid of the evidence. If the guard had seen us, he would have shot us on the spot. I knew he had no idea which prisoner he gave the rucksack to earlier that evening. It was not until after my liberation that I realized we had been drinking German champagne that night, compliments of that SS guard who had probably pilfered the bottles from a Nazi supply house.

Very early the next morning, we stopped at a small railroad station. I am not sure what town it was in, but I believe it was probably the town of Gliwitz. The guards permitted us to sit outside in the snow, and I fell asleep immediately. Later, I felt someone shaking me awake. I got up and boarded a train with the other prisoners. We still had no idea where we were going. Several hours later we arrived at a small concentration camp called Grosse Rosen. We stayed there for a few days, and then the Nazis jammed us into cattle cars on another train.

Again they were moving us, but we still had no idea where we were going.

One of the prisoners on that train with me was a German Air Force pilot who appeared to be in his late twenties. I asked him why he was a prisoner. He told me that the Gestapo had researched his family background and found out one of his ancestors, three or four generations back, had married a Jewish person. Because of that, the Nazis considered him a Jew under their bizarre racial purity theories.

The absolute insanity of the Nazi's "final solution" was clear. It simply did not matter that the Nazis needed all the qualified pilots they could muster at that time. The fact that this pilot probably had a miniscule amount of Jewish blood in his body was enough to have him classified as a Jew and sent to the death camps.

We spent four miserable days and nights crowded in this cattle car with no food or water. Although the train stopped many times during this journey, the Nazis never allowed us to get off. Instead, we remained crammed in together without even enough space to sit or to lie down. It was difficult even to take a deep breath.

I witnessed many atrocities on this train, partly because some of the prisoners appeared to be going mad.

The stench of urine and feces permeated everything. Some prisoners were so thirsty they drank their own urine. Many died of thirst, hunger and exhaustion. A few of us standing on the outside of the crowd were able to stick our fingers out through the cracks in the train, scrape a little snow off the side of the train, and put it into our mouths. Although the snow was moist, it really did nothing to alleviate the terrible thirst. In fact, it seemed to make me thirstier than ever. I could deal with the hunger, but the thirst was almost unbearable.

After what seemed like an interminable journey into hell itself we finally arrived at the infamous concentration camp known as Dachau.

Starvation

Upon my arrival at Dachau, a prisoner whom the Nazis assigned to be our supervisor, met our group. We quickly learned that this person had a reputation for being very brutal in his treatment of fellow prisoners.

We spent approximately two weeks in a quarantine camp inside the Dachau complex. The Nazis then assigned us to live in a "bunker lager," which consisted of a trench cut into the ground covered by a canvas top. We slept on straw sacks that the Nazis placed in the trenches. I assume that the reason we lived in "bunker lagers" was that the main camp at Dachau was overcrowded.

When I arrived at Dachau, I quickly found out that hunger was going to be a much bigger problem than it was at Auschwitz-Birkenau, where my job gave me access to extra food.

At Dachau, all prisoners were on starvation rations. There was absolutely no way possible for me to get extra food, and hunger became my absolute obsession every single day and night.

Shortly after our arrival, I became part of a large group of prisoners assigned to a work detail unloading heavy machinery and equipment that I believe was owned by

Krupp, the German industrial giant. The Germans had moved the equipment from the industrial heartland to keep the Russian Army from capturing or destroying it. The Germans intended to store the equipment on a large estate occupied by a Catholic convent.

To prevent us from trying to escape, the Germans posted SS security guards armed with rifles to watch us. There were anywhere from 200 to 400 prisoners on that work detail. It did not matter how many prisoners it took to do the job because there were always many prisoners available.

The prisoner they assigned me to work with was the same friend I shared the champagne with on our march from Auschwitz. He was a little younger than me and was very clever in finding places from which we could probably steal food. After he discovered a source, I then figured out the best way to steal it without the Nazis catching us.

They assigned my friend and me to a work site close to the convent building. Next to the building was a doghouse with a very large German shepherd chained up next to it. One day, after the nuns had finished their lunch, we noticed a nun bringing a large bowl filled with food out to their dog. The dog seemed very friendly and looked well fed. We stood there in our emaciated condition and watched jealously as that dog ate until he was full. We were so ravenously hungry it was maddening.

I told my friend that we could not let this go on. We had to find a way to steal that food away from that dog.

We found a long stick and put a nail on the end to use as a hook. We decided to hide the stick until we had an opportunity to use it some other day to steal the dog's food. We agreed to tell no one what we had planned to do.

The next day we saw the nun again bring a huge bowl of food out to the dog. When she went back inside the convent, the other prisoner and I made sure that a guard was not watching, then we sneaked up behind some bushes close to the doghouse and used the long stick to pull the bowl away from the dog.

The dog just stood and watched us. Luckily, he never barked or made any sound.

We quickly devoured the food, which tasted like a gourmet meal.

If a guard had spotted us, he would have executed us immediately with no questions asked. But we were never caught.

Somehow, we always managed to be working near the doghouse around noontime. We did not steal the dog's meal every day, although we desperately wanted to. We simply did not want to press our luck and have the guard or nuns catch us. We knew that we had a good thing going, so we limited our thefts to maybe once every two or three days.

After a few weeks, we noticed that the dog was losing weight. We were grateful that he allowed us to share his meals because his food enabled us to have enough strength to continue to exist and accomplish our work details.

One day, we saw several nuns come out and look at the dog. Although we could not hear what they were saying, it was obvious from their expressions that they were probably concerned about their dog getting so thin. They knew they had been feeding him plenty of food, or so they thought.

Once we knew that the nuns were concerned about the dog's loss of weight, we decided that it would not be wise to continue to steal his food.

Now that we no longer had access to the dog's food, we needed to find another source. We never told any other prisoners about our sources of food because we did not want to take the chance of someone informing on us.

My friend and I were working near the convent building another day, and making sure no one was watching, we looked into a basement window and discovered a large quantity of apples being stored there.

We watched that building for a couple of days while we tried to figure out a way to get by the SS guards. I told my friend that we should find some toolboxes and walk right past the guard just as if they had assigned us to work there. We practiced walking past the guard for a few days, heading straight for the basement with the toolboxes on our shoulders. Finally, we decided that the time had come to break into the basement and steal the apples.

An old-fashioned latch secured the basement door. We used our tools to pry the latch open, making sure that it showed no signs of tampering.

Our coats had pockets, but the pockets had huge holes at the bottom. This allowed us to stuff apples into the linings of our coats. We filled the bottoms of our toolboxes, arranging the tools carefully on top, hoisted them onto our shoulders and walked right past the guard. He didn't notice anything.

After we feasted on apples for several days, the guards lined up the entire work detail early one afternoon. It was earlier than usual for our work detail to finish so we became very suspicious that something had to be wrong.

Anytime the usual routine was changed, either in the camps or on the work details, it set off alarms in our heads that something bad was going to happen.

The Nazis lined us up so frequently in the camps and on work details that we developed our own early warning system. Fortunately, my friend and I were in the back row of the formation. One of the prisoners in front heard that the guards were looking for apples, and the word got back to us in seconds.

Communication was critical to our survival, and we learned in the camps to relay words in whispers faster than a telegraph. We were standing there with apples in the linings of our coats. We knew for sure that if the guards found us in possession of those apples, they would immediately kill us.

Within minutes, we passed the apples out to the other prisoners and told them to eat every part. By the time the guards got to us, they did not find a core, seed or stem. It was as if the apples had never been there. The guards dismissed us and allowed us to return to our regular work details. We were simply lucky that the guards who searched us were not the same guards who had observed us going into that basement on a regular basis.

We found out later that the nuns had gone into the basement earlier that day, noticed that some apples were missing, and reported the loss to the SS commander of the work detail.

At that time, it did not bother me because we knew that the Nazis considered their prisoners to be less than insects, not human. However, after liberation I thought back to that incident and sadly remembered that we were turned in by nuns, people who supposedly believed in charity and kindness to the less fortunate of the world.

They knew for certain that we were physically emaciated, that we were forced into slave labor and that we were systematically beaten and tortured, yet they weren't willing to share a few of their apples with us. I have sadly wondered about that ever since.

Each day, when we marched through the town of Dachau to our work site, we passed a huge bakery. The smell of the bread and cakes being baked had a devastating psychological effect on us and seemed to make our hunger that much worse. I often thought how nice it would be if someone would be kind enough to leave a few loaves on the corner for us. It never happened.

For someone who has never experienced real hunger, it is hard to imagine how anyone could eat out of a dog's bowl. However, for us it was simply a matter of survival. We were so hungry that nothing short of death would stop us from stealing that food. We knew that stealing was always a risk, that the Nazis could have shot us for stealing the apples or stealing the dog food. However, we had one goal: survival. It was a known fact of camp life that if you were not willing to take risks, you simply would not survive.

I was willing to risk my life daily because I had no fear. I had no realistic expectation that I was going to survive no matter what I did, so what was there left to fear?

PART FIVE

Liberation

The End is Near

We worked at the convent until the first week of April 1945. We knew that the war was probably coming to an end, that it was just a matter of time.

"The end is approaching, but is it the end for me or for them?" I thought. "Who will make it?"

I definitely did not think I would.

In early April 1945, the Nazi guards moved approximately five hundred of us out of the Dachau concentration camp and placed us on a freight train. I have no idea why they placed us on that train. Whatever their reason, that train then became our prison, complete with guards and dogs. Most of the time the train just sat on the rails because there was no electric power available to move it. Some days, however, the train would move back and forth going nowhere in particular. It did not matter to us whether it moved or not because we were still prisoners.

One day we noticed that we were all alone on the train, with no guards in sight. Five of us jumped off and ran towards the forest. From out of nowhere local politzei (police) suddenly appeared and started chasing and shooting at us. At that time I was in very poor physical shape and was not able to keep up with the other guys. I told them to keep going, that I would stop and let them catch me. The police quickly caught up to me and brought me to a jail where I remained overnight thinking that they would execute me.

Much to my surprise they did not beat or punish me in any way for that attempted escape. I still thought they would shoot me when they got around to it, but the next morning, they just returned me to the train.

At the time, I didn't know if any of the others got away. However, after my liberation, I ran into one of the others, a Frenchman who jumped off the train with us. He had a cast on his arm where the police shot him during the escape attempt. He told me how glad he was to see me because he thought they had killed me after I was caught.

One day, the train was moving very slowly south of Dachau towards the foot of the Alps, somewhere near the town of Seeshaupt.

We heard airplanes approach, and then we heard the sounds of shells exploding into the train. The prisoner next to me had his leg shattered by a shell and later died. Several other prisoners were immediately killed, and many others were seriously wounded.

As soon as the attack started, many of us jumped from the train and ran to a ditch where we remained until the planes flew away.

When I looked up, I saw American markings on the planes. I could not believe that they had attacked us. The Americans must have thought that the train was carrying German soldiers.

A week or so later, still on the train, we looked out one day and saw a large group of soldiers approaching. But these soldiers were wearing green uniforms and green helmets instead of the characteristic metallic gray uniforms and oval helmets of the Germans. After they surrounded our train, we discovered they were Americans.

I distinctly remember the young American lieutenant who was in charge of that unit. He immediately took all the prisoners who were still alive off the train and took us into the basement of a bank building in Seeshaupt. He then ordered the setting up of an Army field kitchen to feed us.

Once this was done, he told me to get into his Jeep and we rode out to a farm where he picked out a prize steer, shot it, had it processed and brought back to the Army field kitchen. United States Army troops cooked the steer and fed it to the liberated prisoners at the bank building. It was a wonderful meal.

While we were riding in the Jeep, the lieutenant sang. I recognized the melody but did not know the words. Through the interpreter I asked him what he was singing and he replied "the Marseilles." I wondered afterward whether he was with the American army when they liberated France.

The next morning the lieutenant picked me up at the bank building.

"Let's go back to the train," he said. For the first time, he saw the horrible conditions, the carloads of dead and seriously wounded prisoners whom the Nazis had left behind. The lieutenant was clearly overcome by the sight of the carnage.

He handed his short carbine to me and turned to his interpreter.

"You have my permission to go into these houses and kill all or as many Germans as you want," he said, pointing to the Seeshaupt village and its residents.

This lieutenant, so emotionally overwrought by what he had seen on the train, had momentarily lost his ability to think rationally.

I handed the rifle back with a shake of my head.

"I haven't killed anyone yet," I told him. "I'm certainly not going to start now."

Return to Life

After several days, the Americans found some trucks and moved several hundred of us into the city of Munich. Many of the other prisoners had already dispersed on their own to other locations.

I did not have any place to go at that time. The Americans put us into an exclusive neighborhood previously occupied by the Nazis. We stayed there for several days.

It was a very peculiar feeling to go from a concentration camp and prison train into such luxury. I am afraid that we did not behave too well while staying there. We smashed glasses against the wall, ate meals off the Nazis' beautiful china and then threw the dishes out the window. I am not proud of those actions; however, it was simply an irrational, emotional reaction to being free after all those years in the camps.

We went a little wild, though we never hurt anyone else with our actions.

After two weeks, an American colonel gathered us together and announced that he was going to move us into a displaced persons (DP) camp. We had had enough of camps. Even though the Americans' intentions were to help us, we couldn't face living somewhere that reminded us of where we had been.

I became angry.

"Hold it right here," I told him. "You're not going to move my friends or me to another camp. You've got two choices, you can move us into housing in Munich or back to Dachau, but we're never going to a DP camp."

A few days later, the Americans moved us into a large, abandoned school building. After we had spent so much time in the camps, where the Nazis controlled every minute of our lives, we found that we were not mentally prepared to handle freedom right away. We had no organization, and had no plans for how we were going to accomplish even the small things in life, such as preparing meals, let alone planning for the future. The Americans just put us in that school and left us on our own to figure out how we could use our newfound freedom. It did not take us long.

After being in the school building for a few weeks, I left with two friends from Ciechanow, David Sobol, and his uncle, Meier. Already I had developed some contacts. I learned that the high commissioner in charge of housing loved opera. He helped us find an apartment, and I rewarded him with opera tickets.

Some German civilians owned the three-room furnished apartment in Munich. They didn't care that we were former prisoners, and we could afford the rent because the housing commission controlled it.

After moving into our apartment, we needed to find some means to earn a living. We engaged in black-marketing and hustling items such as buying and selling watches, jewelry and so forth. Later we became more sophisticated and started trading dollars, marks and other currency. Prices were always fluctuating so you had to be sharp to keep on top of it.

The Search for Simon

The area around the Munich museum was the meeting place where the currency traders gathered to conduct their business.

While engaging in this business I also began my search for clues to the whereabouts of my brother, Simon, or my cousin, Irving. I knew they were not in the Munich area, so I decided to jump on a train and go to Bergen-Belsen to see if I could find out anything about them.

The train went from Munich to Frankfurt and then headed north. Every so often, when the train would halt because of destroyed tracks or a power-outage, I would have to walk to another area to find another train to continue the journey.

After riding on coal trains for a very long eight days I finally arrived in Bergen-Belsen covered with coal soot. After washing my body and filthy clothing, I found some people from Ciechanow who let me live with them for a few days while I searched for information about my brother.

The early days after the war were chaotic throughout Europe.

There was no central source of information available about where the concentration camp survivors were living. You had to find your own clues and do your own searching. One day, while I was standing in the center of town I saw several buses coming in from Czechoslovakia. One of the buses pulled up close to me, and a passenger shouted through the open window.

"Samuel," the man said. "I'll bet you're looking for your brother."

He then told me that he had seen Simon three days before in Prague. I asked him where, and he gave me an address. The former prisoners assemble there every day, he told me.

"You'll probably find him there," he said.

Pleased with this information, I then jumped on another train and started the long trip back to Munich.

When I got home, I told David Sobol my good news and asked him to accompany me to Prague.

"We'll need some type of identification before trying to get to Prague, though," I told him.

At that time, the only identification I had was the number 73538, which the Nazis tattooed on my arm at Auschwitz-Birkenau.

I knew that the Czech officials would need to see some type of identification so I went to a friend, who had been placed in charge of a displaced persons camp in Munich. I knew each displaced person was required to have an ID card with a picture, so I asked my friend if he could make one for me and one for David.

Initially, he told me that it would be impossible to make ID cards for us because we did not live in the DP camp.

"I didn't ask you what you could do for me," I told him. "I told you what I need. I don't care what you have to do. I'll be back tomorrow, and I expect the cards to be ready."

When we went back the next day, my friend was still protesting, but after we talked to him for awhile he took our pictures and issued the phony IDs to us.

Armed with proof of our identification, we then headed for the train station and tried to get on a train bound for the Czech border. After being rebuffed by US soldiers from the occupation Army, we eventually got on a train in Munich that took us into the city of Beyreuth, near the Czech border.

When we got off the train in Beyreuth we immediately found a Jewish person and told him we needed to get to Prague. He told us to cross the Czech border, guarded on both sides by American soldiers, and then get on a train to Pilsen. He warned us to be very careful because the Russians guarded the area between Pilsen and Prague, and they had the reputation for shooting first.

As we thanked him for the information, he took a handful of Czech money out of his pocket, handed it to us and told us to be careful. We each bought a big glass of Pilsen beer, and after drinking it, fell asleep on a bench in the train station.

The next morning, we saw some Jewish people who told us to be very careful not to let the Russian soldiers catch us. They told us to find a train carrying displaced Poles from Germany back to Poland, get on that train and act as if we were also heading back to Poland. Once we found and boarded that train, we spoke Polish to the other passengers and acted just as happy as they were to be returning to Poland.

Of course, we had no intention of going back to Poland. We stayed near the train door ready to jump out if it stopped to take on water or even slowed down while going through the Prague train station. As the train approached Prague, I looked out and realized that it was not going to stop for water, and it was not going to slow down while going through the station.

I told David that we were going to have to jump for it right then, otherwise we would end up in Poland. We both jumped out, rolled a few times and ran into the Prague railroad station. Once we were in the station, we knew that no one was going to bother us. We were able to speak a few words of Czech so we asked for directions to the address where Simon and Irving were supposed to be staying.

After we got on a streetcar, the conductor made a special stop for us and told us exactly where to go. As we walked down the street, someone yelled after us.

"Samuel," the man called. "What are you doing here?"

When I looked up I saw a Polish man who had been in Auschwitz with us.

"I'll bet you're looking for your brother," he said. "I saw him yesterday and gave him some money."

After his liberation, this man had gotten a job working in the Polish embassy in Prague. He knew many of the former prisoners who had settled in the city. He told us just where to go to find Simon, and a few minutes later we found him with my cousin, Irving.

It was like a miracle. The only thing that clouded the happiness of our reunion was our realization that we were the only members of our large family who had survived the Nazis' "final solution."

My brother told me to go into the immigration office in Prague and tell them I was born in Germany and wanted to return. The next morning we walked into the office and told the secretary that we were born in Frankfurt, Germany, and wanted to go back.

She just looked at us for a moment, a sad expression on her face.

"Look," she said. "I've heard that story many times before. I know that you are Polish, so why don't you go back to Poland where you belong. If you don't want to go back to Poland, we'll let you stay here in Czechoslovakia. We'll establish your residence here, and get jobs for you."

In an instant, I decided to confess and tell the truth. I told her that she was absolutely right. We were Polish subjects but we definitely were not going back to Poland and were not staying in Prague either. I told her that I now lived in Germany and had only ventured to her fair city to find my brother and cousin.

Evidently, she liked hearing the truth. She gave me a pass.

A few days later, we all got on the train together and had no problems getting back into Germany.

Financing the Dream

Shortly after returning home, we had earned enough money on the black market to buy a large Mercedes automobile that at one time had been a Nazi staff car. It was in good running condition, had two spare tires mounted on the side of the car, and had green leather upholstery. It was a beautiful car, and we enjoyed driving around in it. We all took turns sleeping in the car to prevent someone from stealing it.

One day a friend told me that he had access to three full sets of brand new Ritter dental equipment and we could buy them for one thousand dollars each. Each set consisted of a dental chair, X-ray equipment and everything else needed to equip three dentists' offices.

After agreeing to the deal, I found some bombed-out dentists in Munich who needed this equipment to furnish their new offices. I told them I wanted gold in exchange for the dental sets. They readily agreed to my terms. After receiving the gold, we immediately exchanged it for American dollars. Needless to say, we made a very fine profit on this deal.

During our time in Munich, we got involved in several other profitable deals that enabled us to live a very high lifestyle.

We did not save any of this money, but we managed to have everything we ever wanted. Later we met some people who brought large sacks full of German marks into Germany from Czechoslovakia. They asked me to be their agent.

Each day I would go to the museum grounds and after agreeing on the exchange rate for that day, I exchanged the marks for dollars. Business was very brisk. We made a reasonable profit because everyone wanted to convert his or her money into American dollars.

After we took our profit, I turned over the remaining dollars to the people who had brought in the sacks of marks. Before long, I became known to the money dealers who immediately raised the exchange rate when they saw me coming. I then had my brother, Simon, or cousin, Irving, act as the dealer, in order to get the best exchange rate.

One of the most profitable deals we ever made was for pencils. After the war, it was very difficult to get pencils and most other commodities. I found a person who needed a very large quantity of pencils, so I went to the Farber plant in Nuremberg and asked to see the plant owner. When I told him what I wanted, he told me that it was impossible to get any pencils. I told him that I would not pay him in marks, but that I would be able to get any materials he needed for his plant.

"Is it possible for you to get some building materials?" he asked me.

I told him that I could. He gave me a list of materials he needed to repair the factory roof, and I took the list to a friend who ran a building materials company in Munich. I asked him what the materials would cost and agreed to his terms. He delivered the necessary materials to the Farber plant and they, in turn, delivered the pencils to me. I then delivered the pencils to my friend Leon Zelkin, who sold them to his contacts in Germany, France and Belgium. We made a lot of money on this deal.

Life in Munich after the war was challenging and exciting. After those years in the camps, we made up for lost time by having as much fun as humanly possible. The one serious goal we had not yet achieved, however, was the goal of emigration to the United States of America.

This was the one thing each of us wanted more than anything after liberation from the concentration camps. Although we were living the good life in Munich, we could not wait for the day when we would go to the United States.

It was like a wonderful dream that we were determined to make a reality.

My cousin, Irving, received permission first to emigrate. His aunt, who resided in New York, agreed to be his sponsor.

My brother and I then received permission to leave Germany.

Sponsored by an international refugee association, we boarded a freighter, the USAT General W.G. Haan, in Hamburg and arrived in Boston on April 19, 1949.

When we arrived on the Boston docks, we had to go through United States Customs.

I must have had a worried, sad look on my face, because the Customs Agent, who knew we had been concentration camp prisoners, took one look at me and called for an interpreter.

I was a stranger in a strange land but the first words I heard in America made me feel wonderful ... and welcome.

"This is the United States of America." he said. "You don't have to worry now because you are among friends."

Those words will stay with me until my dying day.

PART SIX

Epilogue

A Few Final Words

Since coming to America in 1949 I have been asked numerous times if I could ever forgive the Nazis for what they did to me, my family, friends and the others who were murdered in cold blood. I have thought about that question repeatedly and still have not been able to decide. Perhaps I will never be able to make that decision.

I believe that in order for forgiveness to occur, there must be an honest effort by the perpetrators to admit that they were wrong and to ask sincerely for the forgiveness of their victims. In my opinion, the German government and their allies have neither fully admitted nor taken responsibility for the horrors they caused. They have never made a good-faith effort to restore confiscated property, money, paintings, jewelry and other property to their rightful owners. They have never asked their surviving victims for forgiveness. How can there be forgiveness without the perpetrators first fulfilling their responsibilities?

I realize that being able to forgive one's enemies is perhaps a wonderful thing. However, after all the horrors the Nazis subjected us to, I still cannot find the strength and grace to bestow forgiveness on the most evil regime the world has ever seen.

If somehow in the future, I find that I am capable of forgiveness I would only be able to forgive the Nazis for what they did to me personally. I would never presume to forgive on behalf of my father, mother, three brothers, two sisters, many aunts, uncles, cousins, friends, neighbors, and all other innocents who were tortured and died at the bloody hands of the Nazi killers.

While at Auschwitz-Birkenau, I asked, "Where is God?" as I observed the fire raging in the trenches that could have contained and consumed my mother, my sisters and my cousins. More than 50 years later, I no longer dwell on that question because I realize that the horrors of those concentration camps were caused by diabolically evil human beings who were exercising free will.

As I celebrate my fifty second-year anniversary of residing in the United States of America, my adopted country, I thank God for the wonderful opportunities this country has given me.

The proudest day of my life was November 11, 1954, when I raised my hand and took the oath of United States citizenship in the United States District Court, Eastern District of Virginia.

Throughout my more than fifty years as an American, I have consistently tried to live up to the ideals of this country.

I bring closure to this book and to this chapter in my life with a great deal of humility and gratitude. In retrospect, it was my inner-strength and the confidence and belief in myself that helped me survive the Holocaust. While my wounds from concentration camp beatings healed long ago, the wounds that can never heal are the ones inside, in my heart. Yet, I am most grateful that I did endure and have had the opportunity to be productive and to have a meaningful life.

I have a burning love for this country and the soldiers who gave their lives so that I might be free. I have an undying respect for our men in military service.

Finally, I know first hand, that with all of our problems, we have the greatest country in the world.

May God continue to bless America my beloved country.